Oresteia

Aeschylus

Oresteia

Translated, with Notes, by Peter Meineck

Introduction by Helene P. Foley

Hackett Publishing Company, Inc.
Indianapolis/Cambridge

For further information, please address
    Hackett Publishing Company, Inc.
    PO Box 44937
    Indianapolis, IN 46244-0937

    www.hackettpublishing.com

Cover design by Brian Rak and John Pershing.
Text design by Meera Dash and Dan Kirklin.

Oresteia production photographs reproduced courtesy of the University
of South Carolina Theatre: Artistic Director, Jim O'Connor; Director,
Robert Richmond; Set Design, Kim Jennings; Light Design, Ann
Courtney; Costume Design, Betsy Zumfelde.

Cover photograph courtesy of UPI/Corbis-Bettmann

Library of Congress Cataloging-in-Publication Data

Aeschylus.
    [Oresteia. English]
    Oresteia / Aeschylus : translated, with notes by Peter Meineck :
introduction by Helene P. Foley.
        p.   cm.
    Includes bibliographical references.
    Contents: Agamemnon—The libation bearers—The furies.
    ISBN 0-87220-391-3 — ISBN 0-87220-390-5 (pbk.)
    1. Aeschylus—Translations into English.   2. Agamemnon
(Greek mythology)—Drama.   3. Orestes (Greek mythology)—
Drama.   Electra (Greek mythology)—Drama.   I. Meineck, Peter,
1967–   .   II. Foley, Helene P., 1942–   .   III. Title.
PA3827.A7M45   1998   98-37825
882'.01—dc21   CIP

ISBN-13: 978-0-87220-391-4 (cloth)
ISBN-13: 978-0-87220-390-7 (pbk.)

Contents

Introduction to Aeschylus' *Oresteia*   vi

Translator's Preface   xlviii

Diagram of the Stage   li

Cast of Characters, *Agamemnon*   2

Agamemnon   3

Cast of Characters, *The Libation Bearers*   68

The Libation Bearers   69

Cast of Characters, *The Furies*   116

The Furies   117

Selected Bibliography   161

Introduction to Aeschylus' *Oresteia*

Helene P. Foley

Aeschylus, the earliest of the three great Attic tragedians, presented his *Oresteia* at Athens' City Dionysia festival in 458 B.C.E. Born in the last quarter of the sixth century, Aeschylus had fought with the victorious Greeks in one and probably both of the Persian Wars (490 and 480–79). He died around 456 at about seventy years of age in Gela, Sicily. His epitaph records his role as soldier at Marathon, not his artistic achievements, but these were many. The author of more than seventy plays, he won his first of thirteen tragic victories in 484. Of these plays, only seven remain. The *Oresteia* is Aeschylus' only complete surviving trilogy; the satyr play with which it was first performed, *Proteus*, is lost.

Peter Meineck has aimed to translate the *Oresteia* for the modern stage. My introduction will offer a framework for interpreting the trilogy with an emphasis, to the degree that our knowledge permits, on issues relating to performance and production. I begin with two brief sections that set the play in its immediate literary and historical contexts. An outline of what we know about the Greek theatre production, with an emphasis on important issues and controversies about staging the *Oresteia*, follows. My interpretive essay will stress issues that prove particularly difficult for modern performance of the plays: language and translation, the role of the chorus, meter (see the appendix), divine/human relations, and male/female conflict. A final section gives a brief survey of major twentieth-century productions.

The Myth

Despite the trilogy's massive complexity, the story line of the *Oresteia* is not hard to follow. In *Agamemnon*, the king of Argos, Agamemnon, returns home from Troy after ten years of war accompanied by his Trojan slave concubine, the prophetess Cassandra. He is killed by his wife Clytemnestra, who plotted the murder with her lover, Aegisthus. Clytemnestra acts to avenge the death of her daughter Iphigenia, who was sacrificed by her father so that the Greeks could go to Troy. Aegisthus is motivated by revenge as well. Agamemnon's father Atreus had served up Aegisthus' brothers as a meal to their unwitting father Thyestes. Thyestes himself had committed adultery with Atreus' wife in a dispute over the throne. In *The Libation Bearers*, Agamemnon's and Clytemnestra's son Orestes returns from exile to avenge his father at the behest of the god Apollo. After a reunion with his sister, Electra, and an attempt to invoke the aid of his father's ghost, Orestes enters the palace in disguise, kills his mother and Aegisthus, and is finally forced to flee, pursued by his mother's avenging Furies or Erinyes. In *The Furies*, Orestes is purified by Apollo in Delphi but must go to Athens in an attempt to elude the persistent Furies. There the goddess Athena establishes the first trial by jury for murder at the court of the Areopagus. The Furies prosecute and Apollo defends Orestes. The jury is apparently equally divided, and Athena's vote assures his acquittal (the exact nature of the vote remains controversial; see Gagarin 1975, Hester 1981, Sommerstein 1989, Seaford 1995). The goddess then reconciles the outraged Erinyes with a new cult in Athens, and the play closes with a ceremonial procession.

Aeschylus' audience would have been familiar with both the basic outlines of the myth on which the trilogy is based and with earlier poetic versions of it, and thus would have been alert to choices from and changes to the tradition made by the poet. Homer, whose epic poems formed the basis of Attic education, would have been the most familiar source. Homer's *Odyssey* had pointedly compared the tragic homecoming of Agamemnon with the successful return of Odysseus. Whereas Clytemnestra betrays her unsuspecting husband with Aegisthus, Penelope remains faithful to the far more cautious Odysseus, despite the persistent courting of her suitors. Orestes' successful revenge on his father's killers is evoked as a model for their son, the indecisive and youthful Telemachus. We know of other versions of the myth in the post-Homeric epic poems *Nostoi* and *Cypria* (lost except for a few fragments and synopses), in Aeschylus' older contemporary Pindar (Pythian 11), and above all in the Sicilian lyric poet Stesichorus' *Oresteia*, which had an important influence on Aeschylus' version. Stesichorus apparently introduced the figure of Orestes' nurse and Clytemnestra's warning snake dream in *The Libation Bearers* (although the snake in Stesichorus represented Agamemnon, not Orestes), as well as the pursuit of Orestes by Furies and the helping role of Apollo, who in this version gave Orestes a special bow to ward off his pursuers.

Tragedy, however, often differentiates itself from Homeric versions of the myth in its stress on intrafamilial and male/female conflict. The *Odyssey* in no way problematizes Orestes' revenge and does not explicitly mention the matricide. The divisive sacrifice of Iphigenia appears in Hesiod and the epic cycle, but is avoided by Homer; in the epic cycle she is rescued at the last moment by Artemis, who substitutes a deer for the girl. Aeschylus' Clytemnestra herself kills her husband, whereas in Homer she merely slaughters Cassandra. Aegisthus, who plays the active role in Homer, comes on the Aeschylean stage only after the crime has been committed. Aeschylus apparently also highlights the influence of the past crimes of the house of Atreus on the story. Thyestes' seduction of the wife of Atreus and Atreus' vengeful serving of the murdered children of Thyestes (except Aegisthus) to his brother hover significantly over the events of the trilogy. Cassandra's vivid prophecies in *Agamemnon* envision the adultery and cannibalism from the past presiding over and even making inevitable the crimes of the next generation.

Aeschylean adaptations of myth also play a critical role in *The Furies*. In the standard Delphic version of the myth, the god Apollo acquires his prophetic shrine by killing the dragon who guarded the prophetic shrine of Earth or Gaia. Aeschylus' version, in which Apollo's prophetess, the Pythia, tells us that the god received his prophetic powers as a gift from Phoebe (who received it from Themis and Earth), deliberately sets the stage for a peaceful resolution to the repeated violence among members of the House of Atreus. Aeschylus sets Orestes' trial at the site of the Athenian defeat of the Amazons, a group of mythical warrior women who attempted to retrieve their queen from Athens, where she had been abducted by the hero Theseus. Moreover, the Furies or Erinyes are said by Apollo's Pythia to be daughters of the primal female deity Night (no father is mentioned), rather than, as in Hesiod, avenging spirits conceived from blood spattered on mother Earth from the castrated genitals of Zeus' grandfather Ouranos (Sky). Both these mythical choices enhance and finally prepare for a conclusion to the gender conflict central to the trilogy.

#

(Further reading: virtually all commentaries and general studies discuss the mythical background; for detail see Gantz 1993. On Hesiod and Aeschylus, see Solmsen 1949; on visual representations of the myth, see Prag 1985. For gender issues, see esp. Zeitlin 1978.)

The Political Context

The plots of Greek tragedy were generally based on myth rather than reality. Plays on recent historical events, including Aeschylus' own *Persians*, became rare after the early years of tragedy. Indeed, historical tragedies that dealt directly with Athens' own sufferings, such as Phrynichus' *Capture of Miletus*, proved unacceptable. Yet the *Oresteia* remains responsive to the political context in which it was presented. In the fifth century, the mythical war between the Greeks and Trojans often took on the coloring of recent conflicts between Greeks and barbarians, especially the Persians. The Athenian naval empire, developed in the wake of the Persian Wars (490 and 480–79 B.C.E.), was growing rapidly, and bringing new wealth and new influences into the city. (Aeschylus' Agamemnon is repeatedly called "king of ships," an attribute that evokes contemporary Athens more than his Iliadic role as leader of a land army.)

The emerging Athenian democracy had just survived a major political storm in 462–61. The democratic leader Ephialtes, with the help of the youthful Pericles, had succeeded in stripping the aristocratic stronghold of the Areopagus council of many of its powers. (Members of the court had been selected from those who had served as archons; this office was barred to the poorer citizens.) Although it remained a court in which cases were tried involving deliberate homicide, wounding, and arson as well as certain religious crimes, the council now no longer exercised broader powers as guardian of the state and of its laws (this probably included the right to try major offenses against the state and the vetting of magistrates). Its former powers were transferred to the popular courts and to the democratic council. The reforms of the Areopagus generated violent passions. In the process, the conservative statesman Cimon was ostracized and Ephialtes was assassinated.

Given this recent controversy, it is probably not surprising that scholars have been unable to determine Aeschylus' own position on these reforms from his presentation of the mythical founding of the homicide court in the final play of the trilogy, *The Furies*. Exonerated by the court for matricide, the hero Orestes promises that his own city of Argos will never forget its debt to Athens. Contrary to tradition, Aeschylus also locates the house of Atreus in Argos, rather than Mycenae. Orestes' promise is very probably a veiled allusion to a recent alliance contracted between Argos and Athens in 461 that was favored by Ephialtes and Pericles and set the stage for an Athenian challenge to the Spartans for the leadership of Greece. Yet the play's treatment of the Areopagus itself is much harder to interpret along partisan lines. Between them, the Areopagus and the new cult of the Furies founded by the goddess Athena retain the promise to protect the state and preserve it from internal strife on the broadest possible terms that suggest some vague continuity with the Areopagus' earlier mandate. The reform itself had been defended as a restoration of the court's original and proper function. Yet Athena's role in *The Furies* (to say nothing of Agamemnon's in *Agamemnon*) makes clear the importance of leadership to the city, and we should not forget that the entire cast of characters in this debate, including Ephialtes, Pericles, and Aeschylus himself, were of aristocratic background. In praising law and pointedly establishing the court for all time, is Athena implicitly criticizing the reforms, supporting a return to the court's "original" function, warning against further changes, or simply reemphasizing the value of law and political stability in the wake of the recent civil conflict? Members of the audience may well have interpreted the trilogy's conclusion differently. Yet by setting the trial of Orestes at Athens, Aeschylus has given the Areopagus a new founding myth and an enduring importance that more probably suggests a desire to promote reconciliation among factions rather than to take sides and thus to reopen recent wounds.

#

(Further reading: Rosenbloom 1995, Griffith 1995, Meier 1993, Macleod 1982, Podlecki 1965, Dodds 1960, Dover 1957.)

The Theatrical Context

Aeschylus' theatrical genius can be fully appreciated only through an awareness of the context in which these plays were performed. Theatre played a central role in the civic and cultural life of Athens. The City Dionysia, a festival in honor of the god Dionysus at which the *Oresteia* was presented, became under the Attic democracy the most important annual civic festival and a major source of pride for the city. Held in the ninth month of the calendar year (roughly March), when the seas became passable, the five-day event brought many visitors to Athens, including (after 454 B.C.E.) allies bringing tribute that was displayed in the theatre. At least fifteen thousand people were present to observe both the plays and a number of nondramatic ceremonies: sacrifice to the god Dionysus, the pouring of libations by the ten elected generals of that year, the announcement of the names of citizens who had received crowns for benefiting the city, a parade in full armor of orphans whose fathers had died in action and were now to be supported by the polis. The state paid for poorer citizens to attend. Although one probably apocryphal story claimed that the fearful first appearance of the Furies provoked miscarriages among the audience's women, we are not certain whether women were present; most probably citizen wives of childbearing age were least likely to have been present, and women would have represented at best a minority of the audience.

In Aeschylus' time not all of these civic events had yet accreted to the festival. It certainly included dithyrambic contests; each of the ten tribes of Athens entered one chorus of fifty men and one of fifty boys, which sang and danced choral songs on mythological themes in a circular formation. On successive days, three tragic poets each presented three tragedies and one satyr play. Satyr plays featured a chorus of satyrs or goat men, often accompanied by their father Silenus. The major characters of satyr plays were generally mythical deities or heroes, but the unheroic, curious, and vulgar satyrs undercut their tragic dignity. The escapist plots of satyr plays offered a thoroughly Dionysiac release from the sufferings of tragedy. Five comedies were probably performed on a separate day. *Proteus*, the satyr play for the *Oresteia*, dealt with the adventures of Menelaus in Egypt that are familiar from book four of Homer's *Odyssey*. A connected trilogy (or in this case, tetralogy) of related plays seems to have been special to the late Aeschylus, and poets were free to present four unrelated plays.

The City Dionysia was organized by the Eponymous Archon, a civic magistrate who was charged with "granting a chorus" to the poets and appointing a *choregos*, or producer, who financed many aspects of the production, including recruiting, maintaining, training, and costuming the chorus. The city was responsible for the leading actors and poets. The *choregoi* were wealthy citizens who competed for status by displaying their largesse to the city in the form of such liturgies (an indirect tax). We do not know what criteria were used by the archon in selecting the poets. The chorus members (twelve at the time of the *Oresteia*, but later fifteen) and the actors (three for each tragic performance and up to five for comedy, as well as mute extras) were male citizens, who played both male and female parts. The Greek name for actor, *hypocrites* ("answerer" [to the chorus] or "interpreter"), had at this stage none of the negative associations it later acquired and retains in the English derivative *hypocrite*. The poets and their choregoi competed for a prize; victorious poets received ivy crowns; contests for actors were introduced after Aeschylus' death. Ten judges drawn from each tribe were elected by lot to prevent corruption, but audience applause could play a critical role in their decision over the victorious poet.

Dramatic poets were virtuosic artists, who composed both text and music of their plays, directed the performance, designed and rehearsed the choreography, and in the case of Aeschylus and earlier playwrights, acted in their own plays. In *Agamemnon*, for example, Aeschylus, as first actor or protagonist, would have played the part of Clytemnestra. The actor who played Cassandra would have had to be a talented singer. Aeschylus' early plays use only two actors (the second one generally played a messenger role), and the *Oresteia* presents his most sophisticated use of the three actors who became the norm in later tragedy. Because they were masked and performed to a huge audience, actors were especially prized for their command of voice and gesture. Plays were rehearsed for about six months prior to performance, and participants were relieved from military service for this period. Normally, each play received only one performance in the major civic festivals; by 386 B.C.E. tragic revivals were legally permitted, contributing to the canonization of Aeschylus, Sophocles, and Euripides. Revivals of Aeschylus were permitted immediately following his death, and the *Oresteia* was almost certainly among them; both Sophocles' and Euripides' *Electras*, for example, make pointed use of it.

In the open-air Theatre of Dionysus, spectators may have sat on planks in wedge-shaped sections on the southeast slope of the acropolis, with front seats reserved for dignitaries and sections reserved for individual tribes. Our evidence on the details of the seating is too late for any certainty. The *orchestra* or choral dancing space was about twenty meters across and may have been roughly circular, rectangular, or trapezoidal in shape with an altar at its center. Once it was built (probably after Aeschylus' earliest tragedies), the wooden *skene*, or stage building, initially contained at least one central door, and perhaps provided one or two additional playing spaces, the roof of the building (often called *theologeion*) and a wooden stage for actors. Scholars are divided both on whether there was a raised stage at this period and on its height—views range from a low stage about a foot high to one several feet high with steps at the center. We also do not know how far the *skene* encroached into the original orchestral space. Actors and chorus did in any case mingle in the orchestra, whose center would have offered a powerful playing space. The chorus normally entered and exited through two entrance ways (*eisodoi* or *parodoi*) sloping into the orchestra from either side of the stage building, and usually remained there throughout the performance, whereas actors could also enter from the *skene* door. Our manuscripts give no indication of exits and entrances or other critical stage directions, although they are frequently mentioned in the text.

This can create interesting problems for the modern director.
For example, in *Agamemnon*, we do not know when Clytemnestra first appeared on stage. The chorus appears to question her
at lines 83 following, yet she does not reply until its song is over.
Does she make a silent appearance in the background, sending
out servants to make sacrifices throughout the city while the
chorus sings and thus establishing from the outset the powerful
control over the stage and the doorway of the palace that she
maintains until the close of this first play? And where are the
sleeping Erinyes at the beginning of *The Furies*? Choruses usually enter from the *eisodoi*, but this group either comes out of the
central door or is displayed at least in part on a wheeled plat-
form (*ekkyklema*) that could be used to bring out a set tableau
from the interior of the skene, such as Clytemnestra standing
over the bodies of Agamemnon and Cassandra in *Agamemnon* or
Orestes in *The Libation Bearers*, who echoes the earlier scene as he
stands over the bodies of Clytemnestra and Aegisthus.*

Tragic costume became more elaborate throughout the fifth
century (we know nothing about the period at which the
Oresteia was performed); at its conclusion, tragic actors typically
wore a long-sleeved, richly decorated chiton and soft leather
boots. Unusual or grotesque costumes, such as those apparently
worn by the Furies, were more often characteristic of comedy,
and indeed, humorous moments in the dialogue of *The Furies*
have led some critics to wonder if comedy with its bestial choruses is being deliberately evoked by Aeschylus (see Herington
1963 and Lebeck 1971). The tragic mask, covering the whole
head, was naturalistic until the Hellenistic period, when it developed a high forehead and a pointedly downturned mouth.
Both mask and costume enabled the same actor to play characters of different ages and sexes, and a virtuosic first actor may
have wanted the audience to be conscious of the range of roles
he could play, or even to create implicit links between a series of
roles within one play, or in this case, several plays. Props, such
as statues of divinities, seem to have been used from an early
date. Yet painted scenery, said to have been introduced by
Sophocles (his first victory occurred in 468), was minimal, and

---

* A crane (*mechane*) that could be used to suspend gods above the stage
was probably not in use by 458 B.C.E.

could almost certainly not be changed in the course of a play. If Aeschylus used scenery in the *Oresteia*, one wonders how in *The Libation Bearers*, the shift of scene between tomb and palace or, in *The Furies*, between Apollo's temple at Delphi and Athens, with its cult statue of Athena, would have been accomplished.

Above all, one must keep in mind that tragic performance was very much in a state of transition throughout the fifth century. Aeschylus was composing plays in an atmosphere where theatrical possibilities were constantly opening, and poets vied to take advantage of them and create startling new effects. For example, set speeches (*rheseis*) had long been part of the tragic repertoire, but dialogue (*stichomythia*), especially three way dialogue, was at the time of the *Oresteia* at an early stage of development. Even genre boundaries (for example, between tragedy and comedy) were only just emerging with any self-consciousness.

A knowledge of stage conventions built up from observing the remaining tragedies has allowed scholars to speculate on some of the ways that Aeschylus apparently plays on the audience's expectations in the *Oresteia*. To offer a few examples, messengers generally deliver their message immediately and directly. Yet in *Agamemnon*, the messenger is so overwhelmed by his desire to return home alive and anxious not to mix bad news with good that he does not immediately do so. After Agamemnon enters the palace, the audience may well expect, on the basis of other plays, to hear his death cries. Instead, the long scene with the heretofore silent and veiled Cassandra intervenes, and the dignity and heroism of her freely chosen exit to death in the palace contrasts with that of her ignorant and deceived master. Aegisthus' first entrance late in the final scene is also surprising. Clytemnestra's defense before the chorus has concluded, and she has taken responsibility for the crime. Aegisthus' appearance undermines her position and forces her to take on a mediating role between her brash, tyrannical lover and the chorus.

Similarly, the entrance of Orestes' nurse in *The Libation Bearers* is a surprise that effects a sudden change in tone, as she mixes the maternal affection lacking in Clytemnestra with down-to-earth tales of Orestes' babyhood. Furthermore, because ghosts could appear on the tragic stage, some critics have wondered whether the failure of Agamemnon's ghost to appear in *The Libation Bearers* is significant. In any case, gods rarely arrive in answer to mortal prayers in tragedy, and never immediately, as

does Athena in *The Furies*. Apollo, on the other hand, makes an
entirely unheralded exit and entrance in this play. Normally,
when one character is freed from being a suppliant to a god, the
pursuers leave and the suppliant stays. In *The Furies*, the angry
Furies remain while the freed suppliant Orestes leaves. The appearance of divinities on stage thus disrupts normal theatrical
expectations in a fashion that perhaps dramatizes their more
than human and unpredictable nature.

   Greek drama was more operatic than was much later theatre.
Choruses sang and danced their scene-dividing odes, or *stasima*,
and large parts of their entrance and exit songs (the choral exit
could also be spoken or chanted in recitative), accompanied
most typically by a reed instrument, the double pipe or *aulos*.
The music was primarily melodic, and certain modes were
thought to have specific ethical connotations. A limited number
of props and other instruments (e.g., *tympanon* or drum) and
sound effects (e.g., thunder) could be introduced as needed. Actors spoke largely without musical accompaniment in iambic
trimeters, a poetic meter that sounded to the Greek ear closest to
ordinary speech, but they could employ other spoken meters,
sing, or employ recitative either in exchanges with the chorus
(*amoibaion* and *kommos*) or in solo monodies. Our evidence for
the music and dance of drama is confined to representations on
vase paintings, which almost never depict an actual performance, much later discussions of Greek music and dance in antiquity, and a few musical notations on fragmentary papyri. It is
possible, however, that the language and imagery of Aeschylus'
vivid choral odes offer some clue to the ancient choreography.

   Meineck's translation italicizes all the sung parts of the
drama, but cannot indicate those passages presented in recitative. The appendix gives the interested reader some sense of the
trilogy's use of meter as a whole. Aeschylus often achieves important theatrical effects through meter or the manipulation of
choral conventions. In the scene between Cassandra and the
chorus in *Agamemnon*, for example, Cassandra bursts out from a
long, theatrically powerful silence into song. The chorus responds at first in iambic trimeters, but changes meter as it is
drawn into song in response to her intense and puzzling warnings about the future. Cassandra then shifts to trimeters as she
attempts to communicate her prophecies more clearly to the
chorus. Similarly, Clytemnestra begins her scene over the bodies

of Agamemnon and Cassandra in iambic trimeters. The outraged chorus turns to song, while Clytemnestra herself eventually shifts into recitative, a shift that may indicate her increasing
beleaguerement in the scene.

The Aeschylean chorus is normally thought of as a unit, even
if some or all of its spoken lines were delivered by the chorus
leader. Yet when the chorus of *Agamemnon* hears the king's death
cry within the palace, the chorus disintegrates from a group into
twelve separate voices (1346–72). Paralyzed by indecision, it
lives up to its choral role of being largely incapable of any significant physical action (it is not accidental that most tragic choruses are old men or women—see my later discussion of
Aeschylean choruses). In *The Libation Bearers*, much of the scene
in which the chorus, Orestes, and Electra attempt to summon
aid from Agamemnon's ghost is sung, thus creating an atmosphere of high religious intensity that prepares Orestes for the
matricide ahead. Because women, not men, normally impro-
vised such funeral laments, Orestes' participation sweeps him
into an unusual company that perhaps significantly contrasts
with the sober enactment of the trial in *The Furies*. Vendetta justice thus has a different performative mode from the forensic
justice of the court. In *The Furies,* it is the Furies alone who sing,
first as outraged hunters of the criminal and finally as bestowers
of cult blessings on their adopted city of Athens.

#

(Further reading: for staging of the *Oresteia*, see Taplin 1977. On
staging generally, see Pickard-Cambridge 1968, Simon 1982,
Rehm 1992, Csapo and Slater 1995, and Wiles 1997. On Greek
music, see West 1992; on dance, see Lawler 1964. For vase paintings that may relate to dramatic performance, see Trendall and
Webster 1971.)

Justice in the *Oresteia*

Any reader of the *Oresteia* will immediately grasp its central
theme: justice. The plot itself encompasses an historical transition from vendetta justice to institutionalized trial by jury. Yet
for Aeschylus, this transition involves far more complex issues
than the founding of a new civic institution by the goddess

Athena in Athens. Justice is a political issue, but without the cult of the Erinyes, the institution cannot stand. Justice requires reimagining both divine/human relations and the social and economic order, including the structure of families and the relations between male and female. The central issues posed by each crime in the House of Atreus can only be communicated through language and symbol. Yet language and symbol are shown to be ambiguous, unreliable, or even dangerous tools of communication that can at best be tamed only by the divine persuasion of Athena. (From epic poetry on, only divine speech was thought to have a direct relation to truth.) Although many modern readers have questioned the *Oresteia* for its perhaps overly facile resolution and for its sexual politics, it is hard to argue that Aeschylus fails to dramatize the trilogy's central issues with a compelling vividness and subtlety. Although the drama itself engages justice on all of these levels simultaneously, my own discussion will offer a framework for interpreting the trilogy by looking separately at its politics and economics, language and imagery, and the treatment of divine/human and gender relations. A brief section on interpreting Aeschylean choruses will follow.

The Politics and Economics of Justice

Aeschylean justice is ultimately dependent on a particular social and political structure. *Agamemnon* takes place under a monarchy and *The Libation Bearers* under a tyranny, in which Clytemnestra and Aegisthus rule Argos against the will of its people and deprive Orestes and Electra of their heritage. The change of setting in *The Furies* underlines the impossibility of establishing a just society with either earlier form of government. This insight corresponds directly to Athens' own sense of its history. Once ruled by mythical kings, it had proudly overthrown tyrants in the last quarter of the sixth century. *The Furies* does not directly refer to the democracy that emerged thereafter. Athena presides over a seemingly leaderless Attic society, yet lays the foundation for the world familiar to Aeschylus' audience. Greek myth and thought linked tyrants with women, both because a rule imposed illegitimately on the people prevents the well guarded and secluded tyrant from indulging in the freedom of movement characteristic of a free man and because tyrants are inevitably tempted to indulge appetites in a fashion characteristic of women and barbarians, both of whom are thought to be naturally undisciplined. By making the tyranny over Argos de facto a rule of Clytemnestra, Aeschylus exploits these parallel cultural assumptions about women and tyranny.

Difficulties posed by *Agamemnon*'s monarchy are represented in a more complex fashion. The chorus, though critical of the king, nevertheless views Agamemnon as a source of legitimate authority. Yet monarchy dangerously intertwines the interests of family and city. The theft of the adulterous Helen by Paris leads the brothers Agamemnon and Menelaus to a war with Troy that proves devastating to the population of Argos and provocative of civic unrest. At stake here are what one might call ancient principles of international relations, which depended on the rules of hospitality and the host-guest bonds violated by Paris and presided over by the greatest of Greek gods, Zeus. At the same time, however, the virgin goddess Artemis, who presides over the young from birth to marriage and maturity, demands the sacrifice of Agamemnon's daughter, apparently as a sort of restitution in advance for the killing of a pregnant hare that represents in part the innocent lives lost in the capture of Troy. Agamemnon's public responsibilities immediately provoke controversy within his own household, as Clytemnestra, in anger over the death of her daughter, takes up with Aegisthus and plans a revenge on her husband. Yet Clytemnestra's revenge turns her against her own children. Conflict within the household encompasses the state.

Monarchy is also vulnerable to corruption through its concentration of power and wealth. Agamemnon's victorious army may exact justice from the Trojans, but in their greed for the spoils of war they violated the shrines of the gods. As Agamemnon arrives on stage in a chariot with Cassandra, the chorus sings that

> *Justice shines her light*
> *on humble, smoke-filled homes,*
> *honoring the righteous man.*
> *The gold-encrusted palaces*
> *where the hands of men are tainted,*
> *she abandons with eyes averted.*
> *She has no respect for the power of wealth ... (773–81)*

Not surprisingly, then, the king soon succumbs to walking on the crimson tapestries sacred to the gods that Clytemnestra spreads before him as if he were an oriental monarch. The color of the tapestries symbolizes both the blood spilled between Agamemnon's departure for Troy and his return and the wealth of his household. Clytemnestra closes the scene with a reference to the inexhaustible wealth of the household and the highly expensive purplish red dye used to stain its fabrics (959–60). Soon, she gloats that this very wealth will support her own and Aegisthus' claim to power.

In *The Libation Bearers*, Orestes has been raised in exile, apart from the potentially corrupting wealth and power that he nevertheless wishes to reacquire as his due. He remains, however, motivated to commit matricide above all by the divine commands of Apollo. This gradual diminution of the effects of wealth and power on the human pursuit of justice prepares us for the final play, in which justice is taken out of the hands of the family group and placed in the hands of a jury of neutral citizens. This separation of public and private worlds leaves wealth to benefit the society as a whole, and the riches promised by the Eumenides in their new cult is above all natural: flocks, crops, and children. In Homer's *Odyssey*, the presence of a good and just king produced these same benefits (19.108–14). The world of democratic Athens, however, no longer trusts even the virtuous monarch to guarantee them.

Justice, then, requires the subordination of family and kinship to the interests of the state as a whole and a separation of public and private interests. These ideas are expressed visually as well as verbally. The action moves away from palaces and enclosed spaces to public ones. In *Agamemnon*, characters are lured to destruction within the haunted House of Atreus. In *The Libation Bearers*, Orestes and Electra reestablish family bonds outside a palace that has now become an armed camp haunted by guilty dreams; Orestes, pursued by the Furies, must leave the palace for exile in the concluding scene. In *The Furies*, Apollo's shrine is besieged by the Erinyes. Yet in Athens the action occurs entirely in the public spaces of the city, and the Furies accept seclusion in a public cult. *Agamemnon* vividly displays the concentration of wealth in the palace. Sacrifices radiate out from it to the city. Agamemnon appears high above the level of the chorus in a chariot. We cannot know whether the spoils of war prominently accompany him or if his dress has been touched with Asian splendor. Clearly, however, Clytemnestra and Aegisthus, accompanied by henchmen, rely on this wealth to maintain their power. In *The Furies*, the once ominous color of the tapestries is echoed in the crimson cloaks donned by the reconciled Erinyes; in the Panathenaic festival at Athens resident aliens (metics) wore cloaks of this color. The Furies' capacity for bloody vengeance is tamed to serve the larger social order. Pomp and circumstance are visibly transferred to the city, and citizens dominate the stage in this celebratory closing procession.

#

(Further reading: Dover 1957, Dodds 1960, Jones 1962, Podlecki 1965, Macleod 1982, Meier 1993. On the closing procession, see Headlam 1906 and Herington 1986.)

Language and Imagery

Justice is also a product of language and logic, of the relation of words and arguments to reality and truth. Both sets of murders and the three "trials" of the trilogy—the defenses of Clytemnestra and Aegisthus before the chorus, of Orestes before the chorus at the close of *The Libation Bearers*, and of Orestes at Athens—all depend on verbal persuasion. The repeated efforts by the mortal choruses to comprehend justice and divine/human relations depend entirely on words. Aeschylus' use of language in the *Oresteia* can be described only as extraordinary. Dense, ambiguous, and experimental, especially in the choral odes, it poses exceptional difficulties for audience and translator alike. His style is rich with striking and often mixed metaphors, vivid imagery, and complex periphrases that sometimes make ordinary events strange and almost inaccessible. The poet invents new words (especially compound adjectives), borrows obscure ones, and fractures ordinary syntax. Long sentences of loosely linked clauses alternate with occasional pithy nuggets of traditional wisdom. Sentence fragments or sentences that shift construction midway abound in the choral odes. The following passage from Anne Lebeck's groundbreaking study of the trilogy makes clear the interpretive problems involved in Aeschylean language even for the classical scholar:

It should be a basic principle in interpreting Aeschylus that when language and syntax are most difficult, the poet has compressed the greatest number of meanings into the smallest possible space. Pursuing the customary methods of classical scholarship one is sometimes tempted to treat ambiguity as if the author were at fault, as if the clarity of normal diction were beyond his grasp. Yet that ambiguity characteristic of Aeschylus is not easy to achieve: it comes about neither by accident or inability, but by design.

Commentaries on the *Oresteia* sometimes degenerate into arguments about the "right" meaning of passages where wording is enigmatic and meaning multiple. The following approach is here pursued: when argument arises over meaning, the statement that claims to be exclusively right is categorically wrong. The philologist should not restrict himself to a single interpretation of such passages but should give free rein to all possibilities and associations, ultimately selecting as many as form part of a larger pattern and contribute to the meaning of the total work. The linguistic devices by which ambiguity is effected should be analyzed and the significance of the passage then interpreted in the light of its obscurity (p. 3).

What is the poet aiming at with this complex poetry? For the reader in translation, following the trilogy's dense nets of imagery offers the most accessible clue to the working of Aeschylean language. Imagery involving light and dark is, for example, pervasive in the trilogy. The *Oresteia* begins in darkness, as the watchman waits for a light to come from Troy. It arrives but does not bring the salvation hoped for by the city. In *The Libation Bearers*, Orestes, the putative "light" of salvation, ends the play under siege from the Erinyes, forces of darkness. It is only in the confrontation staged in *The Furies* between the Furies and the Olympian gods of the upper world that clarification emerges and unstable polarities break down. As Eumenides ("Kindly Ones"), the dark, angry Furies will still provoke fear, but they will also send up fertility to earth and city. The trilogy closes as the Eumenides are accompanied with a torchlight procession to the world below.

Forces of entanglement are also central to the trilogy as a whole. In determining to sacrifice his daughter, Agamemnon puts on the yoke of necessity; Iphigenia herself is muzzled from speaking by a bit (234). Troy is curbed (132) and forced to adopt the yoke of slavery (529). In *The Libation Bearers*, Orestes goes mad as he looks at the robes in which Clytemnestra snared Agamemnon in the bath. In *The Furies*, he escapes finally from the curbs, bits, snares, and nets that have tripped up all not only individual characters in the trilogy but also whole cities. Other complex repeated images, such as lions, snakes, blood, or disease, all work to suggest the impossibility of capturing the meaning of events except through metaphor; yet in the final play, these same images are again used to create a sense of release and at least greater clarity.

The world of *Agamemnon* is dense with the ambiguous language of dream and prophecy. The words of the prophets Calchas and Cassandra are only partially understood by those around them. The House of Atreus is haunted by Menelaus' image of Helen (412–26) and the pitiful dead children of Thyestes (1217–18). Similarly, Clytemnestra's bad dream sets the stage for *The Libation Bearers*. The aged chorus of *Agamemnon*, whose members characterize themselves as like a dream in daylight (82), struggles to emerge from a nightmare of past, current, and future events that it cannot control. Its words repeatedly suggest ominous realities that it cannot grasp. The audience, of course, knows the myth and can uncover some of complexities inaccessible to the characters, but is nevertheless forced to confront a prophetic nightmare of its own. The very words that it uses to interpret and control the world are running amok. Too many meanings are present. Let me give one extreme example. At line 137 the chorus is reporting Chalchas' interpretation of a portent that appears as the Greeks set out for Troy: two eagles tear apart a pregnant hare and provoke the anger and pity of the goddess Artemis. The difficult Greek text (*autotokon pro lochou mogeran ptaka thuomeoisin*) could be translated either as "sacrificing the pitiful hare together with her young before birth" or as "sacrificing a pitiful female, his own child, on behalf of the army." Calchas interprets the sacrifice of the hare by the eagles, who represent Agamemnon and Menelaus, as predicting the successful capture of Troy. Yet lurking within this promise of success is another sacrifice that will bring terrible sorrows to the pair, that of Iphigenia. In a similar fashion, the story of the gentle lion cub that grew up to turn on its foster parents (718 ff.) at first seems to apply only to Helen's coming to Troy. Yet once lion imagery has been applied to the other main characters in the trilogy (Clytemnestra, Aegisthus, Agamemnon, Orestes, and the Furies), it becomes impossible to isolate any one person or event from the other. The savagery of the house of Atreus is infectious, spreading through a chain reaction that links past, present, and future.

Even the most seemingly neutral gesture has ominous undertones. At *Agamemnon* 92–95, for example, the chorus questions Clytemnestra as to why she is having sacrifices performed around the city. They describe the process of making the sacrificial flames burn more brightly with special unguents as follows (here I offer a more literal and less elegant translation than Meineck's in order to bring out particular ambiguities in the Greek):

alle d'allothe ouranomekes
lampas anischei
pharmassomene chrimatos hagnou
malakais adoloisi paregoriais

And from this side and that as high as heaven
a torch sends up its light,
charmed by the holy unguent's
soft guileless coaxing.

This uncanny flame hyperbolically reaches up to the abode of the gods at whom it is aimed. Yet the unguent is "charmed" or "drugged" (*pharmassomene*) to burn by a persuasive force (*paregoriais*) suggestive of both speech (words of consolation or encouragement) and of medicine. The word "guileless" (*adoloisi*) applies appropriately to an unadulterated substance and a speech "without deceit"; yet the negative "*without* deceit" also suggests its opposite. These soft (*malakais*) coaxings belong best, due to the general implications of the term, to women or barbarians. On the one hand, Clytemnestra's celebratory gesture at the news from Troy is appropriate to her role as priestess. Yet this ambiguous description prepares us for the chorus' unease at the queen's confidence in the message of the beacon from Troy and at female speech itself, which they later describe in terms that

could mean either "too credulous (*pithanos*, 485), the boundary
of a woman's mind is easily encroached upon by rapid inroads"
or "a woman's ordinance, too forcefully persuasive, spreads
abroad, traveling swiftly" (see Denniston and Page 1957). *The
Libation Bearers* reiterates the fundamental impossibility of
proper and reliable communication between men and women,
especially in a public context. Orestes asserts that the respect or
reverence owed by a man to a woman obscures the exchange of
speech; a man can speak clearly and confidently only to another
man (665–67).

In the first two plays of the trilogy, those who sense the fundamental ambiguity of human communication, and the divine
power lurking beneath quotidian reality, can try to harness these
forces to serve their own ends through wishes, prayers, curses,
and verbal gestures. In *Agamemnon*, the persuasive speech of
Clytemnestra repeatedly exploits these possibilities and endows
her, temporarily, with an almost uncanny authority that is reen-
forced by her control of the palace door. For example, Clytemnestra gives two speeches about the beacon announcing the
Greek victory. In the first, she describes its route from Troy in
hyperbolic language that turns the flame into a nearly cosmic
force; she then, unnoticed by the chorus, brings the fires that destroyed Troy metaphorically down on the House of Atreus itself
and thus verbally performs in advance the revenge she plans:

until, at last, it struck the roof of this House of Atreus,
a flame akin to its Trojan ancestor. (310–11)

The chorus is unconvinced by her speech and wants to hear it
again. Clytemnestra then vividly describes the horrors of the
sack of Troy, but warns that impiety and greed during the sack,
the dangers of the return sea voyage, or the malice of the dead
may yet taint the victory. This speech is uncannily prophetic and
ominous (the Greeks have or soon will encounter all three of
these dangers). Yet the chorus simply finds it persuasive—even
masculine in its wisdom (351). We are thus not surprised when
Clytemnestra's outrageous and finally persuasive speech in the
famous tapestry scene with Agamemnon proves able to overcome her husband. Here she first upstages him with a shameless, public description of her private sufferings as wife during
his absence as her handmaids spread purple tapestries before

his chariot, thus attempting to prevent him from entering the palace without trampling on cloths sacred to the gods. Then she persuades him to do so against his will.

Even Clytemnestra's opening speech to Agamemnon (855–913) is fraught with ambiguity to an audience who knows that she is deceiving him. Her description of the messages that she received about Agamemnon's supposed death on the battlefield, which describe him as pierced with more holes than a net, hints at the crime she is about to perform. Her exhausted grief and her anxious waiting for the beacon express other motives beyond those of bereft wife. Finally, and most outrageously, she offers an extravagant, Asiatic welcome to her husband that pointedly borrows imagery from the reunion of the faithful Penelope and Odysseus in the *Odyssey*. "The strong [lit. grounded] pillar of the towering roof" recalls Odysseus' famous bed, built around a tree that holds up the roof of his house; "the one true heir to his father" fits Odysseus, not Agamemnon, who has a brother; and the image of "the sight of land to shipwrecked sailors" is borrowed from a simile that marks the recognition of Odysseus and Penelope at *Odyssey* 23.233–40. Although the audience dwells on the disparity between Clytemnestra's false self-presentation as faithful wife and that of the cautious and true Penelope, Agamemnon notes only the length of his wife's speech and its inappropriate praise. Fully conscious that the act of stepping on the tapestries is transgressive, he capitulates to his persuasive wife in a mere fourteen lines. Her speech deflects Agamemnon by urging him to be true to his principles and then undermining them with a series of unlikely hypotheses that culminate in a female plea to the conqueror hard to resist after her public show of suffering and the choral reminders to the king of the people's unhappiness over the war. Clytemnestra thus publicly demonstrates Agamemnon's willingness to imitate the oriental ruler Priam and the corruption of the king since his departure to Troy. She closes the scene with a plea to Zeus to fulfill her prayers (973–74); the audience knows that the object of these prayers is the successful murder of Agamemnon.

Clytemnestra's speech overcomes both the chorus and Agamemnon. Yet Cassandra's resistant silence proves intractable; once the prophetess speaks, we see the limits of the queen's verbal authority. Cassandra cannot be believed by the chorus; but her speech captures the full complexity of the troubles of the

House of Atreus, and the interconnections between past, present, and future opaque to Clytemnestra, who harbors illusions, by the end of her later self-defense to the chorus, of making peace with the evil demon haunting the household (1570–76). In *The Libation Bearers* it is Orestes who now deciphers the queen's dream of the snake that draws blood from her breast and who turns language with all its ambiguities against his mother. In *The Furies* the goddess Athena applies persuasion to a new end, the establishment of law court and cult that claims to serve the interest of the whole state and of peace and stability rather than violence or individual desires.

Understanding the language and imagery of the *Oresteia* is an immense theatrical resource for the modern director and choreographer. Greek tragedy is not realistic drama. Its characters are created to serve the larger action, and we are not invited to psychologize them beyond what is readily apparent in their words and gestures. Yet both the multileveled language and imagery used by chorus and characters and the choral song and dance permit expressing the complexity of an imagined world in which every aspect and event is interconnected to others through a different set of theatrical means.

#

(Further reading: Knox 1952, Peradotto 1964 and 1969, Lebeck 1971, Betensky 1978, Rosenmeyer 1982, Goldhill 1984 and 1992, and McClure 1997a and b. On characterization in Greek drama, see Easterling 1973 and Gould 1978.)

Divine/Human Relations

In the *Oresteia*, justice cannot be achieved without the help of the gods in founding a new civic institution at the Areopagus and a new cult of the Erinyes. Greek religion is above all a matter of cult performance: sacrifices, libations, festivals, and prayers to the gods. Sacred texts, whose interpretation belonged to a priestly class, played virtually no role. Theology was the province of persuasive citizens, but above all of poets who interpreted, reinterpreted, and modified a body of traditional myths about gods and humans, often in public performances before the city. Especially in *The Furies*, for example, Aeschylus bor-

rows from and reinterprets the archaic cosmological poetry of
Hesiod; his views of justice also closely echo the poetry of the
early Attic statesman Solon. The *Oresteia* presents a struggle to
understand the justice of Zeus. Yet even by the celebratory conclusion of the final play, the ways of the gods and their justice
remain mysterious and not entirely satisfactory.

Justice, at least in *Agamemnon* and *The Libation Bearers*, might
better be termed revenge. The archaic Greek morality of "do
good to your friends and bad to your enemies" predominates.
Yet each act of retribution, however justified, demands its price,
and the chain of violence finds no end. As the chorus puts it in
The Libation Bearers (310–13):

> *Justice screams*
> *and demands her price.*
> *Bloody blow pays bloody*
> *blow. "The doer suffers,"*
> *sounds the saying, three times old.*

The chorus in *Agamemnon*, struggling in its "ode to Zeus"
(160–83) to understand a divine justice that is sometimes long
delayed in coming and not always from the mortal perspective
clearly "just" in its workings, can only propose that by Zeus'
law mortals must learn by suffering (176–78), that "discretion
comes even to the unwilling" (180–81), and that divine grace
comes violently (182–83).

In *Agamemnon*, communication among gods and mortals is
ruptured, distorted, and corrupted; as the trilogy evolves, however, communication is reestablished. The implications of the
prophecy of Calchas in *Agamemnon* are only partly understood
and cannot save mortals from crippling choices and errors; Cassandra's warnings go unheard, as the chorus struggles hope-
lessly to play the prophet itself (975–83). Her knowledge cannot
prevent her death. Agamemnon is apparently directed by Zeus,
the god who presides over the relations among hosts, guests,
and strangers, to avenge Paris' violation of Menelaus' hospitality in the abduction of Helen. The kings become a fury against
the transgressors (59). Yet this command demands not only the
inauguration of a war fought for an adulterous woman, but also
the sacrifice of the innocent Iphigenia demanded by Artemis.

Then Agamemnon, the eldest, spoke:

> *"An unbearable fate will fall on me if I disobey*
> *but how can I bear to slaughter my own daughter,*
> *the glory of my House?*
> *How can I stain my hands, the hands of a father,*
> *with this young girl's blood, as it drenches the altar?*
> *How can I choose? Both ways are full of evil!*
> *Should I desert the fleet and fail my allies?*
> *The sacrifice stops the storm,*
> *the blood of a virgin must be spilled,*
> *rage craves rage,*
> *what must be must be.*
> *Let it be for the best."* (205–17)

How can Zeus' justice encompass the apparent divine conflict between Zeus and Artemis? Does it consistently require the making of choices in which each alternative is both right and wrong? All actions in the first two plays of the trilogy appear so overdetermined by divine forces, the past, and heredity that the human struggle toward justice seems at first bound to fail.

In *The Libation Bearers* Orestes attempts to follow the command of Apollo at Delphi. The word of the god seems clear. Yet this command requires Orestes to murder his own mother and pollute himself with her blood. Apollo cannot stave off the pursuing Furies even after he has purified Orestes at Delphi. His ritual proves visibly ineffective as the sleeping Furies awaken immediately after the purification and take off after the fleeing Orestes. Even Clytemnestra, who is neither provoked to act directly by signs from a divinity nor presents her act as a choice between two necessary goods and evils, claims religious authority for her act. She not only acts to avenge her daughter, but she also claims that her crime descends from the spirit of vengeance in the House of Atreus (1497–1504), which began with the crimes committed in the previous generation by Atreus and Thyestes and perhaps even earlier with Pelops and Pleisthenes (1568). Here her self-defense anticipates that of her lover Aegisthus, who takes revenge on Agamemnon for Atreus' crime against his father and brothers. Yet it also echoes the vision of Cassandra, who links each act in the household to its past crimes.

At the opening of *The Furies*, prophecy is restored to its traditional place. The Pythia believably represents the word of Apollo and justifies his acquisition of his prophetic shrine at

Delphi in terms that eliminate the violence and ambiguity in the traditional myth. The warring gods come on stage to present their positions in person, and Athena mediates between them. The court and the cult of the Erinyes are founded in divine presence. Yet even here, the word of Zeus is not clear. Apollo claims that his argument represents his father's will (616–21); he wishes to ignore the justice represented by the Furies. Athena, however, finds a place for them and echoes not only the argument of Apollo, but the words of the Erinyes. Is she, then, the true representative of Zeus? Can Zeus' justice obtain only at Athens? Furthermore, the jury on the court founded by Athena is evenly divided over Orestes' matricide. Without Athena's vote Orestes would not have been acquitted and the court could not have resolved the problem posed by vendetta in the House of Atreus. Can human judgment reliably reflect the justice of Zeus in the future? The cult of the Erinyes makes clear that the law courts alone cannot be relied on. The fear that they instill will deter men from committing crimes, and they will move into the breach once again if the justice of mortals falters. The concluding procession, by foregrounding the cult of the Eumenides and upstaging the civic institution, puts justice back at least partly into the hands of the mysterious gods, whose words will no longer be heard so directly.

The struggle to understand and communicate with the gods takes on its most theatrical dimension in the trilogy's representation of ritual. *Agamemnon* opens with sacrifices of thanksgiving performed throughout the city. Yet we know that Clytemnestra's rites imply more than gratitude. Cassandra calls the bath in which the queen will kill the king a *lebes* (1129), a sacrificial cauldron used for boiling meat. Clytemnestra herself later represents her killing of the king as a sacrifice, yet her description of the act distorts and misuses the rite, thus suggesting a corruption of proper communication between gods and humans and of the social order (1384–92):

> I struck him twice and he screamed twice,
> his limbs buckled and his body came crashing down,
> and as he lay there, I struck him again, a third blow
> for Underworld Zeus, the savior of the dead.
> He collapsed, gasping out his last breath,
> his life ebbing away, spitting spurts of blood,

which splattered down on me like dark sanguine dew.
And I rejoiced just as the newly sown earth rejoices,
when Zeus sends the nourishing rain on the young crops.

At a Greek banquet, the third libation of wine is poured to Zeus. Here Clytemnestra makes Agamemnon's blood the third libation that will produce fertility for the land from her body. Yet her perverted and highly sexualized murder/sacrifice echoes the perverted meal of Thyestes' children, the sacrifice of Iphigenia, and the "sacrificial" killings at Troy (65, 136).

Human sacrifice is itself the perversion of a ritual in which animals are normally substituted for humans. Unlike Iphigenia, the sacrificial animal assents to its death by being made to bow its head. Agamemnon kills his innocent daughter like a beast, with apparently brutal indifference to her cries. And as we saw from the passage above, the very process of making the decision to kill her is overwhelmed by the desire of the army (and Agamemnon himself) to go to war. His act of piety becomes an act of impiety.

> And as he strapped himself to the yoke of Necessity,
> his storm-swept psyche veered on an impious course,
> impure, unholy, unsanctified.
> At that very moment he changed
> and his altered mind would dare do anything.
> Such shameless thoughts make mere men bold,
> maddening minds and reducing them to ruin.
> And so he dared to sacrifice his daughter,
> a first offering to bless the fleet,
> to fight that woman-revenging war. (219–27)

The beginning of *The Libation Bearers* enacts a long ritual appeal to the ghost of Agamemnon that requests support for Orestes' enactment of the command of Apollo. Piously performed, even this ritual is not without ambivalence. Legislation at Athens outlawed non-kin from lamenting at tombs, as the chorus of foreign female slaves does here. And such lamentation was probably strongly associated with vendetta justice (it is traditionally used in many cultures to stir up relatives of the dead to take revenge). The chorus tries to instill in Orestes the rage that will ensure his act. Electra herself is unsure whether she can

ask the gods to repay evil with evil (122), and wishes to maintain "the discretion my mother lacks" and "keep my hands clean
and pure" (140–41). In the end, Orestes does not act in anger,
nor is his killing described as a "sacrifice." Indeed, without the
intervention of Pylades, who has been silent up to this moment,
and who now reminds Orestes of Apollo's command (900–902),
he might not have been able to act. Orestes maintains his doubt
about the matricide, yet he soon becomes the marked sacrificial
victim of the Furies.

It is not surprising, then, that the trilogy must close with a
restoration of ritual, and hence of proper communication between gods and men. The Erinyes will accept sacrifices (1037)
and give fertility in return. They must be continually pacified,
but will try to keep their worshippers pure of heart. The trilogy
opens with prayers for salvation from the watchman. The beacon comes, but the light it brings is also destructive. *The Libation
Bearers*, too, opens with a series of prayers to Hermes and the
ghost of Agamemnon. Yet Apollo cannot protect Orestes from
the Furies. All the gods answer prayers in *The Furies*: the Erinyes
those of Clytemnestra, Apollo those of Orestes, and Athena
those of Orestes and Athens. But although ritual is vividly enacted as an effective channel of communication to the gods in
the final civic procession, the question of justice remains more
complex.

This issue has been particularly well articulated in the work of
Simon Goldhill (1984, 1986, and 1992), and I will only sketch the
complexities here. The Greek word for justice, *dike*, means not
only justice and right, but retribution, punishment, law-court,
and law case. All these meanings come into play here, and once
again excess of meaning threatens to destabilize any sense of
resolution. As the characters struggle to pursue justice in this
trilogy, *dike* paradoxically clashes directly with *dike* (*LB* 461).
How, then, can *dike* be justice? *The Furies* creates an institution to
resolve the issue. Yet, as we saw, the institution of legal justice
cannot solve Orestes' dilemma without the intervention of
Athena.

Moreover, the social obligations imposed on humans by the
gods and their own morality can come into irresolvable conflict.
War is one obvious arena where lines are hard to draw. Does the
trilogy find a solution to the problems posed by Iphigenia's sacrifice and the war at Troy? Later in the same century the poet

Euripides expressed his doubts on this last point. In his *Iphigenia among the Taurians*, half the Furies, dissatisfied by the verdict, continue to pursue Orestes; Orestes can return home only after voyaging to the far reaches of the Black Sea, where he finds and brings back to Attica both his sister Iphigenia—who in this version was rescued from sacrifice by Artemis to be her priestess in a remote country— and the statue of the goddess. Their return is nearly prevented by a gigantic wave stirred up by the sea god Poseidon, whose wrath over Troy has not yet relented.

Finally, as twentieth-century Marxist and feminist critics have stressed, the justice offered in *The Furies* privileges the interests of the male and the state. Hence it is difficult for a modern audience to perceive and accept it as justice.

#

(Further reading: Kuhns 1962, Kitto 1956 and 1961, Lloyd-Jones 1956 and 1971, Whallon 1980, Goldhill 1984, 1986, 1992. On ethical choice, see Peradotto 1964, Hammond 1965, Lesky 1966, Dover 1973, Edwards 1977, Nussbaum 1986. On Aeschylean character, see Easterling 1973 and Gould 1978. On ritual, see Zeitlin 1965 and 1966 and Lebeck 1971.)

Male/Female Conflict

In the *Oresteia*, justice ultimately requires the political disenfranchisement of the female but offers her a separate role in cult. In *Agamemnon*, the chorus comes to Clytemnestra "respectful of [her] power." "It is just," they continue, "to honor the wife of a ruler when her husband's throne is vacant" (258–60). Clytemnestra is in charge in her husband's absence. Even on his return she continues to dominate the public space with her speech, and when she has avenged herself on him, she takes power with her lover Aegisthus. The language and action of the trilogy make clear that, despite her lip service to Aegisthus as ruler, the androgynous Clytemnestra is the dominant partner, the male to his female. She kills the king and later looks for an axe to defend herself against Orestes in *The Libation Bearers*. It is she who answers the door to the disguised Orestes when a man or male servant would have been expected. Yet the Erinyes who represent her cause in *The Furies* are finally excluded from the law courts, although they win honors in cult. This resolution reflects reality in classical Athens. The Areopagus court, like all political institutions in Athens, was exclusive to male citizens, but women played an important role in the religious life of the city.

Apollo's counterintuitive "scientific" argument in defense of Orestes' crime claims that Orestes is not biological kin to his mother. The male is the true begetter of the child, while the mother merely nurtures his seed. This reflects one of several views of conception prevalent at the time (it is later confirmed by Aristotle in his *Generation of Animals*), although it fits classical reality more loosely. Inheritance in Athens was in fact bilateral, although the paternal line took precedence over the maternal one. Athena supports Apollo's view with a mythological argument about her own birth. In Hesiod's *Theogony* we are told that Zeus swallowed Athena's pregnant mother Metis ("Cunning Intelligence") to prevent the birth of a male child who would unseat him. Metis' female child was then born from Zeus' head. Because she was born from her father alone (her argument elides Metis), Athena gives precedence to the male in everything except marriage (737), although she demonstrates much more respect for the Furies and their claims than Apollo.

This argument appears arbitrary and even absurd to a modern audience, and it may even have seemed so to some in its original one. After all, half the jury does not accept it. Moreover, because Apollo himself originally loses an argument based on mythical precedent with the Furies and is thus forced to turn to "science," arguments from myth have already taken on a certain arbitrary character. Apollo appeals to the authority of Zeus and rightful kingship to make the murder of Agamemnon look more important than that of Clytemnestra. The Furies challenge Zeus as precedent in this case; after all, he chained up his own father, Cronus (641). Chains, Apollo counters, can be loosed, but shed blood is irrecoverable. That is exactly the problem with your defense of Orestes' crime, reply the Furies. How can a polluted matricide live in Argos? In Greek tragedy, characters are responsible for their crimes even when constrained to perform them by a god and by the ethics of a system of justice that predated the legal alternative of a trial. Orestes acted intentionally. Yet by Attic standards he could not be exonerated legally. Hence his acquittal must in a sense depend on a divine intervention, just as the trilogy itself could not conclude in a fashion that countered contemporary realities in the relations between the genders.

Froma Zeitlin has categorized the *Oresteia* as a "myth of matriarchy," a cross-cultural category of myth that affirms male social dominance by imagining that women once held power, but rightly lost it by abusing their authority. Although Clytemnestra has just claims against her husband, she also kills the rightful ruler of the country, establishes an unjust tyranny, and turns in fear of revenge against her own children. The figure of the nurse in *The Libation Bearers* exposes her lack of genuine maternity (despite Clytemnestra's original championing of Iphigenia). In *Agamemnon*, Cassandra inaugurates the process of making a monster of Clytemnestra (1231–37). The chorus in *The Libation Bearers* puts the queen in a long list of mythical female monsters who killed sons, fathers, or husbands (585–651). Orestes' killing of his mother is linked to the beheading of the gorgon Medusa by the hero Perseus (831). Indeed, critics have argued that Orestes' pursuit of matricide takes on the coloring of a male initiation ritual, in which the son must violently separate himself from his mother and be reborn in the world of men through the purification rites of Apollo. Finally, Clytemnestra's representatives, the Furies, are visually repulsive and terrifying —withered virgins in black, dripping blood as they hunt their prey and seek to suck the blood out from Orestes' body. The contrast with the beautiful, youthful Apollo and the armed maiden Athena could not be more pointed. The Furies and their fearsome and nurturing powers cannot, as Apollo wishes, be excluded from Athens, but they must agree to be subservient to the state that honors them and to dwell underground and out of the civic space of the city.

We should not forget, however, that the female is not the only or even the original source of disruption in the House of Atreus. Behind the present troubles lurk not only the adultery of Atreus' wife but also the abuses of children by their male relatives—the murdered children of Thyestes and the sacrifice of Iphigenia— and male lust for power and war. The image of Orestes as snake or lion links him with the world of beasts as well. The resolution of *The Furies* would have been impossible without the suppression of the unjust death of Iphigenia in *The Libation Bearers* and the idolizing of the all too human king of the first play by his children in the second. (Iphigenia is mentioned once by Electra

at 242, but not as a blot against Agamemnon, and Clytemnestra
does not use her example in defending her crime to Orestes.) *The
Libation Bearers* also sets the stage for the trilogy's resolution by
bringing the male Orestes into alliance with the female Electra,
and by stressing the similarity between them in the recognition
scene. At the same time, the properly virginal Electra, unusually
for a major character, departs from the stage in mid-play and
leaves the action to the men. Normal Greek gender relations
thus gradually begin to reemerge after the inversions and hos-
tile polarities disrupting them in *Agamemnon*.

The Furies and Clytemnestra act in the interests of kin, re-
gardless of the effects of their actions on marriage and civic
order. Indeed, in *Agamemnon*, Helen and Clytemnestra revolt
against the institution of marriage (which subordinates the
woman), and even Cassandra has rejected masculine sexual
domination by refusing Apollo. Cassandra, by assenting to and
then reneging on a promise to give herself to the god, is punished by having her prophecies disbelieved; by contrast, the
aged Pythia of *The Furies* is the faithful servant of Apollo. The
Areopagus is pointedly located at the spot where the Athenians
defeated the female Amazons, who rejected marriage and lived
apart from men. At the same time, Agamemnon himself shows
his insensitivity to his wife by returning after so many years
with a mistress, Cassandra, whom he asks Clytemnestra to welcome. It is thus not surprising that in *The Furies* Apollo stresses
the importance of the marital relation and that the ancient virgin
goddesses, as Eumenides, agree to accept sacrifices for marriage
and watch over the birth of healthy children. By the close of the
trilogy marriage, sacrifice, and agriculture, the central institutions of the civilized world in Greek myth, are simultaneously
reinstated and normalized. Athena's androgyny differs funda-
mentally from that of Clytemnestra and the Amazons. As a permanent virgin, her sexuality poses no threat. Ever her father's
daughter, both Athena's weapons and her persuasive speech
serve marriage and the state.

\#

(Further reading: Winnington-Ingram 1948, Harris 1973, Bamberger 1974, Gagarin 1975, Zeitlin 1978, Rabinowitz 1981, Goldhill
1984 and 1992, Vidal-Naquet 1988, McClure 1999, Foley 2001.)

Interpreting Aeschylean Choruses

Greek drama is thought to have grown out of choruses, with the first actor either imported from outside or developing out of the role of chorus leader. Choral performance was a central part of Greek civic life. It introduced youth into the culture and its myths and prepared men for the synchronized group movement critical to Athenian military life. The ambivalent relationship between a group and its leader(s)—sometimes dependent, sometimes in conflict—was also critical both to the tragic plot and to the political life of Athens. Yet choruses are a relatively unfamiliar part of modern drama, and modern performances of Greek tragedy tend to be at a loss both in staging them or in understanding their role. The difficult language of choral odes (especially difficult in the case of the *Oresteia*), which operates on different terms from the spoken portions of the play, compounds the problem.

Aeschylean choruses are central characters, in constant dialogue with the principals, and verbally resistant or supportive even if they do not act. Partly because they rarely act, choruses are most often old men past military age or women, or those at the margins of Attic political life. (Divine choruses like the Erinyes in *The Furies* are more active than human ones.) The choruses of the *Oresteia* are particularly true to their role throughout. At the same time, they are witnesses, often expressing traditional wisdom, or viewing the action in broader historical or theological perspective. As the philosophers of justice in the trilogy, they struggle and fail to construct fully satisfactory explanations for what they experience; at the same time, their understanding can be more limited than that of the actors. They pray, grieve, and bring the past to bear on the present; often free from obligation, they can withdraw from involvement or express fear and compassion. They set the stage for the coming action, shape audience expectations, and link episodes (and in this case plays) with their repeated themes and images.

In *Agamemnon* each separate choral song is shorter than the one before. In each the chorus begins with the hope of making sense of its world, and ends in despair at comprehension. The entering song (*parodos*) begins with a confident assertion. Agamemnon and Menelaus are described in language that suggests litigants in a law suit (*antidikos*, 41); they are, so to speak, prosecuting Paris for Zeus. A word play in line 41 (*dithronou dio-then kai diskeptrou*) on the Greek words for "two" (*di-*) and Zeus (*dios*) link the two kings and the god of hospitality. Yet the ambiguity and complexity of the play's poetic world immediately begins to emerge in the first simile, which compares the army departing for Troy with vultures who circle above a nest now emptied of nestlings. In contrast to Homer, where simile and reality remain separate, the simile's birds and ships merge: the birds have children (*paidon*, 50; the word is normally applied to humans), their wings row like oars; it is for the birds (now linked with the kings) that the gods send an avenger. The late appearance of the Fury (59) is stressed by placing it last in the sentence, a poetic effect possible due to the inflected nature of the Greek language. Because Greek nouns have different endings reflecting their function in a sentence (here the object), Greek poets can use word order to emphasize ideas. In the simile the loss of Helen becomes one with the loss of children, thus ominously linking the advent of the war to past and future losses of children, both in the House of Atreus and elsewhere. Finally, the "just" war inaugurated by Agamemnon and Menelaus becomes anonymous "wrestlings" over a promiscuous woman that destroy both sides equally. The army is now a congregation of mere struggling bodies: knees and spearshafts. Nothing can assuage the wrath that has been generated (62–71).

In the parodos, the chorus, after breaking off to identify itself and question Clytemnestra's sacrifices, returns to the ambiguous prophecy of Calchas about Troy discussed earlier. Its distress and confusion over how this prophecy, which foretells both victory and sorrow for the House and seems to pit Artemis against Zeus, leads to a meditation on Zeus' justice. The chorus then returns to the events leading up to the sacrifice of Iphigenia and closes with a horrifying description of the father callously indifferent to the death of his innocent daughter. Once again it repeats its sense that Dike "will tip the scales, to bring learning through suffering" (250–51), and that humans cannot control the inevitable. Iphigenia's sacrifice sets the stage for the (re)appearance of her brooding avenger, Clytemnestra.

The next choral ode, the first *stasimon* (a song delivered once the chorus has taken up its position in the orchestra), follows Clytemnestra's two beacon speeches and reflects a similar movement from confidence to uncertainty. Zeus has punished Paris and Troy. Yet as the chorus meditates on the departure of Helen, who brings a disastrous "marriage" to Troy, its thoughts turn to the abandoned Menelaus, haunted by the image of his lost wife, and to the men lost in the war, who return as ashes in urns. The city is angered over the loss of its young men. Finally, the ode concludes with the chorus's wish to be neither a captor of cities nor a captive, as well as with its renewed doubts about the truth of the beacon. The following scene with Clytemnestra and the herald confirms the fall of Troy, but it also raises new doubts.

The second stasimon, which follows the scene with the herald, assures the chorus that the city is taken, although at the cost of much suffering described by the herald. The chorus begins by meditating on the name of Helen. Its root, *hel*, links the name to words meaning "destroy." Helen's hellish name uncannily suits her historical role. Once again the chorus reviews the errors of Paris, both specifically, and then more philosophically. Its image of justice breeding injustice is rich with the language of birth and inheritance that begins to broaden its implications and link it as well with the crimes of the House of Atreus. Agamemnon probably enters just at the point that it concludes that justice dwells only in the houses of the poor and righteous.

In its last independent stasimon, which follows the tapestry scene, the chorus is full of anxiety. Its meditations on justice and revenge are generalized, as if even it can no longer separate the Trojan enemy from those at home. From then on, the chorus confronts Cassandra, lapses into indecision when it hears the king's death cry, and finally confronts his killers, Clytemnestra and Aegisthus. Although it is helpless to defend or mourn its king, it introduces fresh doubts into the minds of his killers. Unusually for Greek tragedy, Clytemnestra, not the chorus, has the play's last lines, reflecting her control of the action throughout and now her acquisition (despite growing anxiety) of civic power.

The chorus of black-clad female slaves of *The Libation Bearers* enters to identify its role as female mourners and avengers. The chorus's dark clothing prefigures that of the Erinyes, and in this play it in a sense embodies the Furies of the dead father Agamemnon, as it supports his children, takes the initiative in inciting their anger, and even helps to deceive the returning Aegisthus. In the *kommos*, the choral song and movement shared by the chorus and the children, the group of avengers becomes one. Even the masks link them, for the youthful and probably beardless Orestes and Pylades no doubt have masks similar to those of the women. More youthful than the chorus of *Agamemnon*, this chorus is a group of active lamenters, who beat their breasts, tear their hair, pour libations, and beseech the king's tomb. A more lively choreography may well have set the pace for the rapid action of the second part of the play. In *The Libation Bearers*, the remaining odes closely follow the action, with the exception of the ode on female monsters mentioned earlier, and reflect once again on the nature of justice both divine and human.

The increasingly active role of the chorus in *The Libation Bearers* comes to a climax in the chorus of Furies. The sleeping Furies, awakened by the ghost of Clytemnestra, probably enter in disarray from inside the shrine of Apollo (a highly anomalous choral entrance), and then rush off stage in pursuit of Orestes. When they arrive at Athens they sing a "binding" song in which they try but fail to paralyze their victim with their speech. In classical Athens, archaeologists have unearthed many "curse tablets" on which litigants inscribed curses by which they hoped to bind the tongues of their opponents in law suits. The Furies make a similar attempt with their magical song. Their leaping movements reinforce their excited rhythms. In their next ode on justice (490–565), they echo the traditional wisdom of the choruses of the first two plays, and assert that the middle way between despotism and anarchy is best. Although Athena sides with Apollo on the question of Orestes, she echoes this ode of the Erinyes closely in the speech in which she establishes the Areopagus court (esp. 690 ff.), thus preparing for her later mediating role. Following the trial, the Furies turn from wrath to beneficence towards the land of Athens, a shift echoed in a gradual change of meter (see the appendix).

#

(Further reading: Rosenmeyer 1982 has a good general discussion of Aeschylean choruses; see, more generally, Wiles 1997. On curse tablets, see Faraone 1985. See also the further reading for the section on language and imagery.)

The *Oresteia* and Modern Performance

Although much studied in the twentieth century, the scale and complexity of the *Oresteia* pose many difficulties for the modern director. Among notable productions were those of Jean-Louis Barrault (1955), Vittorio Gassman with Pier Paolo Pasolini (1960), Tyrone Guthrie (1966), Karolos Koun at Epidauros (Theatro Technis, 1980 and 1982), Peter Stein in Berlin (1982), and then elsewhere, Peter Hall at the National Theater in London (1981; a video recording is available from Films for the Humanities), and Ariane Mnouchkine's Théâtre du Soleil in Paris (1990). A notoriously nationalistic Nazi version directed by Lothal Müthel was performed during the Olympic games at the State Theater in Berlin (1936). Andrei Serban staged an *Agamemnon* in New York (1977). Discussions of two less well-known productions by John Chioles at Stanford University and by Nicholas Rudall at Chicago's Court Theater (1986) are available in Chioles 1995 and Grene and O'Flaherty 1989. (Grene and O'Flaherty did the translation.) An adaptation by Suzuki Tadashi, *Clytemnestra*, was first performed at the Toga festival in Togamura, Japan, in 1983. John Barton and Kenneth Cavender's *The Greeks* (Aldwych Theatre, London 1980) presented a cycle of Greek myth from Homer and parts of nine Greek tragedies, including the *Oresteia*, that has been performed worldwide. Other important adaptations or remakings of the trilogy include Eugene O'Neill's *Mourning Becomes Electra* (1931), T. S. Eliot's *The Family Reunion* (1939), and Jean-Paul Sartre's *The Flies* (*Les mouches*, 1943). Martha Graham's brilliant dance version, *Clytemnestra*, has been performed periodically by her company since 1958.

Both Koun's production and Tony Harrison's highly inventive translation for the Hall production made a point of creating a primeval world out of which enlightenment could emerge from darkness. Koun's masks and costumes (designed by Dionysis Fotopoulos) formed the backdrop for the terrifying performance of Melina Mercouri as Clytemnestra. Harrison's translation for Hall's highly stylized production uses trochaic meter, heavy Anglo-Saxon alliteration, and neologisms such as "he-god" and "she-god." Both the all-male cast, who used full masks, and the translation drew the audience's attention to the trilogy's "sex war" (as Harrison puts it) and reminded the audience that it represented a male view on justice. Mnouchkine's four-play trilogy (the *Oresteia* was preceded by Euripides' *Iphigenia in Aulis*) also emphasized gender issues. Euripides' play, for example, developed strong sympathy for the wronged mother and daughter before the trilogy began. Martha Graham's *Clytemnestra* focuses on a female perspective by representing the myth from the queen's point of view.

Stein's production (in the tradition of Max Reinhardt's *Oedipus Rex* and *Oresteia* [Munich 1911]) used a prose translation and no music and choreography. The audience sat on the floor, and the chorus moved on a path through it. Among the most brilliant theatrical moments were the opening cries of Cassandra, emerging from a tentlike veil covering her entire body; as the prophetess explains (lit., unveils) her cryptic prophecies, the actress emerges from the veil and begins casting off her clothes. In *The Libation Bearers*, Orestes' argument with Clytemnestra (brilliantly performed by Edith Clever) evolved with his sword to her naked breast. In *The Furies*, the Furies' wrath literally blasts the jurors, sending them into immediate battles among themselves. Athena then shows her respect for the transformed monsters by leading each by hand, dressed in their highly symbolic crimson cloaks, to a post at the base of the stage.

Both Suzuki's adaptation and Mnouchkine's tetralogy demonstrate the value of Asian theatrical traditions for the staging of Greek tragedy. The influence of Indian Kathakali and Japanese Kabuki and Noh on Mnouchkine's staging, music, and choreography were brilliantly successful during the choral dances. The ambitious choreography, large choruses, and music played on a range of instruments drawn from many traditions proved electrifying. The words of the odes were chanted by a single voice between dance sequences and had little impact, however. Despite the brilliant spectacle, the production in general showed insufficient respect for the text in the staging. For example, the Furies (a group of three bag ladies and a pack of dogs) sang their threatening binding song to an Orestes who was inexplicably offstage.

Suzuki's script is a composite of scenes from the *Oresteia*, Sophocles' *Electra*, and Euripides' *Electra* and *Orestes*. Drawing on Noh and Kabuki, traditions that like Greek theatre used masks, male actors, poetic language, and heroic settings, it deliberately mixed different historical periods and put eastern and western traditions in tension. In performance, Orestes spoke

English and dressed in modern western clothes, while the other characters spoke Japanese and dressed in Noh or traditional Japanese costumes. Electra, caught in the middle, spoke Japanese but wore western dress. The staging stressed the isolation of modern (especially western) man (Orestes) and the collapse of a family overly dominated (in both Japan and Aeschylus) by the mother. West infects east, yet eastern familial piety makes the western justice of Greek drama impossible. In the final sequence, Clytemnestra, played by the brilliant Shiraishi Kayoko, returned as a Noh ghost and killed her two westernized children.

#

(Further reading: Taplin 1989, McDonald 1992, Hartigan 1995, Burian 1997, and Macintosh 1997.)

Appendix on Meter in the *Oresteia*

Dialogue in Greek tragedy is generally conducted in a poetic meter thought to be closest to ordinary speech, iambic trimeter. Greek meter does not depend, as in English, on rhyme or stress but on quantity, that is, on patterns of long and short syllables, with long syllables held twice as long as short ones.* Iambic trimeters are composed of three metrical units in which limited substitutions of two short (**u**) syllables for one long (**-**), or one long for a short are permitted: **x-u-** (where **x** means that a long or two shorts can be substituted for the usual iambic **u-**). Thus the first line of *Agamemnon* would be scanned as follows:

u - u - -   - u - u - u -
theous men aito tond' apallagen ponon.

Aeschylus occasionally uses another spoken meter, trochaic tetrameters (**-u-x -u-x -u-x -u-**), for stressful moments such as the debate of the chorus after the murder of Agamemnon or the conflict between Aegisthus and the chorus at the end of *Aga-*

---

*Ancient Greek also had a pitch accent in which the voice either rose a certain interval or rose and fell on specific syllables. Pitch accent operated in counterpoint to the metrical system.

memnon. This meter was associated with the earliest Greek tragedies.

Passages chanted in recitative—between song and speech— use an anapestic meter (**uu-**). The chorus of *Agamemnon* uses this meter, which was linked with marching, for its entrance. The basic anapestic unit is **uu- uu- uu- uu-**, occasionally abbreviated as **uu- uu-**. A dactyl (**-uu**) or spondee (**- -**) can be substituted for the anapest (**-uu**).

Aeschylus uses a rich range of sung lyric meters in the *Oresteia*. These can combine iambs (**u-**) and trochees (**-u**), with variations called cretics (**-u-**) or bacchiacs (**u- -**); dactyls (**-uu**); choriambs (**-uu-** with variations called, for example, glyconics); ionics (**uu- - uu- -** with variants such as anacreontics, **uu-u-u- -**); or dochmiacs (**x- -u-** with frequent substitutions of **uu** for **-**). Of these meters, dactyls and dochmiacs pick up the pace. Dactyls may occasionally have epic associations (see *Agamemnon* 104–59), inasmuch as Homeric epic is composed in dactylic hexameter; the closing dactyls of *The Furies* underscore the celebratory release of the conclusion. Dochmiacs are consistently linked with moments of high excitement, tension, or suffering. William Scott has argued that a particular trochaic colon called a *lekythion* (**-u-u-u-**) is thematically linked with the justice of Zeus, whereas iambs are associated with sin and punishment. Although aspects of this argument have been questioned (see Chiasson 1988), the unusual frequency of *lekythia* in the *Oresteia* may well have thematic implications.

The sung parts of choral odes usually involve two repeated metrical units called *strophe* and *antistrophe* (meaning "turn" and "counterturn" because of the choreography accompanying the song) that are sometimes followed by a refrain or different metrical unit (epode). Each pair of strophes and antistrophes has a different metrical pattern. We do not know whether the music or choreography was the same for each, but they may well have been. If so, choreography and music must in some way link each pair (see Wiles 1997, esp. p. 96, for further discussion).

The choral entrance song in each play is called a *parodos*, the exit song (or speech) an *exodos*. Any scene-dividing ode sung with the chorus already on stage is called a *stasimon*. In practice, however, these odes generally bridge scenes, and should not be viewed as separate from them despite the formal shift from speech (or speech and song) to song.

The following scheme identifies all meters other than iambic trimeter in each play of the trilogy.

Agamemnon

Parodos (choral entry song)—lines 40–103 anapests (recitative); 104–257 sung (104–59, mainly dactylic with iambs; 160–91, trochaic; last section mainly iambo-trochaic). Lines 160–91, which include a "hymn to Zeus," have many lekythia.

Stasimon 1—355–488 sung (lyric iambs, some choriambs).

Stasimon 2—681–781 sung (trochaic, variations on glyconics, iambics, ionics, anacreontics); 782–809—chanted anapests by the chorus to the entering Agamemnon.

Stasimon 3—975–1034 sung (mainly trochaic; then dactyls, cretics, iambics; then cretics, anapests, dactyls; then trochaic with dactyls).

The Cassandra scene—1072–77. Until 1119, Cassandra sings and the chorus uses iambic trimeter. (This represents reversal of the usual situation, where a chorus may sing but characters speak). Then both Cassandra and chorus sing. The meter in this scene is mainly dochmiacs. At 1178 Cassandra shifts to iambic trimeter. 1331–42—chanted anapests by the chorus between Cassandra's exit and Agamemnon's death cry. 1343–47—trochaic tetrameters for the choral indecision after the death of Agamemnon.

Chorus confronts Clytemnestra—1407–11 and 1426–30 (lyrics, mainly dochmiacs); Clytemnestra replies in iambic trimeter. 1448–1566—the chorus sings (iambic and aeolic, then iambic; mainly anapestic lyric refrains intervene between strophe and antistrophe) and Clytemnestra replies in chanted anapests at 1462–67, 1475–80, 1497–1504, 1521–29, 1551–59, 1567–76. 1649–end—trochaic tetrameters. The chorus confronts Aegisthus while Clytemnestra tries to mediate.

The Libation Bearers

Parodos—22–83 sung (lyric iambics); chorus 152–63—astrophic song (lyric iambs and dochmiacs).

Kommos (lamentation at the tomb of Agamemnon)—315–475

(the exact distribution of lines is not certain here, for the manuscripts did not originally indicate who spoke or sang which parts). The lyric meters here are largely choriambic with some iambs. The chorus opens and closes the *kommos* with the less intense chanted anapests, while the children sing throughout.

306–14 chanted anapests (chorus)

315–22 strophe 1 (Orestes)

323–31 strophe 2 (chorus)

332–39 antistrophe 1 (Electra)

340–44 chanted anapests (chorus)

345–43 strophe 3 (Orestes)

354–62 antistrophe 2 (chorus)

363–71 antistrophe 3 (Electra)

372–79 chanted anapests (chorus)

380–85 antistrophe 4 (Orestes)

386–93 strophe 5 (chorus)

394–99 antistrophe 4 (Electra)

400–404 chanted anapests (chorus)

405–9 strophe 6 (Orestes)

410–17 antistrophe 5 (chorus)

418–23 antistrophe 6 (Electra)

424–28 strophe 7 (chorus)

419–33 strophe 8 (Electra)

434–38 strophe 9 (Orestes)

439–43 antistrophe 9 (chorus)

444–50 antistrophe 7 (Electra)

451–55 antistrophe 8 (chorus)

456–60 strophe 10 (Orestes, Electra, chorus)

461–65 antistrophe 10 (Orestes, Electra, chorus)

466–70 strophe 11 (chorus)

471–75 antistrophe 11 (chorus)

476–78 chanted anapests (chorus)

Stasimon 1—585–652 sung (largely iambo-trochaic with lekythia interspersed).

Stasimon 2—783–837 sung (largely trochaic with some ionics); 855–68 chanted anapests by chorus between Aegisthus' exit and his death, followed immediately by 869–71—sung (dochmiacs and lyric iambics).

Stasimon 3—935–71 (largely dochmiacs).

Exodos—chorus at 1065–76 (chanted anapests).

The Furies

First parodos—143–78 sung (iambo-dochmiacs).

Second parodos—254–75 largely sung (astrophic—dochmiacs with a few iambic trimeters).

Stasimon 1—sung 321–96 (mainly trochaic with lekythia, then dactyls; finally iambic).

Stasimon 2—sung 490–565 (mainly trochaic with lekythia, then dactyls; finally iambic); chorus 778–880—sung (iambo-trochaic and dochmiacs); chorus 916–1020—sung (iambo-trochaic with many lekythia and dactylic).

Exodos—1032–47—dactylic exit sung by escorting chorus.

\#

(Further reading: Scott 1984. All major commentaries offer metrical analyses. Lloyd-Jones 1979 offers much help for those without Greek.)

I would like to thank Nancy Worman and Charles Barker for their comments on an earlier draft of this essay. —H.P.F.

Translator's Preface

An early version of this *Agamemnon* received its first public performance at the Lillian Baylis Theatre, Sadlers Wells, London, in 1991. The first reading of the entire *Oresteia* was held at Columbia University, New York, in 1997 by the members of the Aquila Theatre Company. A shortened version of the text was staged at the University of South Carolina in 1998. The text is based on the editions of Eduard Fraenkel (*Agamemnon* 1950), J. D. Denniston and D. L. Page (*Agamemnon* 1957), A. Garvie (*Choephoroi* 1986), Sommerstein (*Eumenides* 1989), and A. Podlecki (*Eumenides* 1987).

My main objective in undertaking this translation of the *Oresteia* has been to produce a work that is accessible, performable and dramatic while retaining a fidelity to the Greek. For those with little knowledge of Greek drama I have sought to create a translation that transmits the power, passion, tension, and beauty of the Greek in a form that is both immediately understandable and dramatically compelling. I have not attempted to re-create the meter of the Greek, preferring a rendering of the English suited to the oral delivery of an actor on stage. However, I have placed sung passages in italics and indicated strophic response to give the reader a sense of Aeschylus' all-important dramatic form and structure. All in all, I hope this volume will help promote an appreciation of Aeschylus' superb trilogy to the widest possible audience, both on the page and on stage.

The Greek texts have come down to us without stage directions. Opinions about these have always been controversial and are bound to remain so. Yet, I feel strongly that one of my responsibilities as the translator of a play text has been to make informed decisions about stage movements. I have done this based on the experience of staging Greek drama at both Delphi and Epidaurus and in hundreds of modern performance spaces of all shapes and sizes. One benefit of this experience has been an appreciation of the profound effects of masked acting for stage movements. The opportunity to work with actors proficient in mask, use them in rehearsal and performance, and contribute to a fully masked production of the *Oresteia* at the University of South Carolina, has proven invaluable in forming my opinions on this subject.

An understanding of the culture and society for which a play was originally conceived is essential to comprehending the work, and in turn, the creation of a faithful performance. To this end I have included brief footnotes intended to create a frame of reference for the trilogy without detracting from the flow of the text itself. Helene Foley's Introduction provides an excellent background to the world of this play, and readers interested in digging deeper will benefit from her detailed bibliography.

I would like to thank the many people who have proved a positive influence in the creation of this work, particularly the members of the Aquila Theatre Company who first performed *Agamemnon*: Lloyd Notice, Graham Mitchell, Julie Kate Olivier, Antonia De Sancha, Kevin Howarth, Peter Hilton, Dee Canon, and Peter Bull. Robert Richmond, Artistic Director of the Aquila Theatre Company from 1993, has been a constant source of support culminating in his excellent production of the *Oresteia* at the Drayton Theatre, with the students of the Department of Theatre Speech and Dance at the University of South Carolina. My time at USC has been made fruitful and rewarding due much in part to the generous support and encouragement of Jim O'Connor, Peter Sederberg, Ward Briggs, and Thorne Compton as well as the enthusiastic students of the South Carolina Honors College in my Greek Drama and Classical Greece classes.

My grateful thanks also go out to Kurt and Deborah Boedecker and the staff of the Center for Hellenic Studies in Washington, D.C., who awarded me a Summer Fellowship in 1997 that enabled me to complete much of the scholarly work on this manuscript. Dirk Obbink and Graham Mitchell helped guide me through the original production of *Agamemnon*, and I cannot thank enough the army of committed and passionate teachers of classics who have time and time again moved heaven and earth to bring the Aquila Theatre Company to their campuses and local theatres. My teachers at University College London had a profound and positive effect on my appreciation of Greek culture and drama, particularly Pat Easterling and Alan Griffiths.

I would also like to thank Brian Rak and Jay Hullett at Hackett for their unflinching support and innovative ideas and Robert Ketterer of the University of Iowa for his excellent suggestions for improving this text. This work is dedicated to my parents, Margaret and David Meineck.

Peter Meineck

Diagram of the Stage

Schematic reproduced courtesy of Courtney/Collins Studio. Copyright 1998

Hypothetical reconstruction of the Theatre of Dionysus, circa 458 B.C.E. (according to Meineck). In the orchestra are uncostumed blocking mannequins, as seen from approximately ten tiers above the first seating row (seating not shown). Scholars are divided both on whether there was a raised stage at this period, and, if so, its height. For more information on the Theatre of Dionysus, tragic costume, and other aspects of the theatrical context, see the Introduction.

Agamemnon

Beware, for Artemis, pure goddess, feels pity.   (134)

Cast of Characters

WATCHMAN	for the House of Atreus
CHORUS	of Argive elders
CLYTEMNESTRA	queen of Argos
HERALD	of the Argive army
AGAMEMNON	king of Argos
CASSANDRA	a Trojan captive, daughter of King Priam
AEGISTHUS	cousin of Agamemnon and lover of Clytemnestra
SERVANT WOMEN	of Clytemnestra
BODYGUARDS	of Aegisthus

Agamemnon

SCENE: *The House of Atreus in Argos. Nighttime.*

(A disheveled watchman appears on the roof of the house.)

WATCHMAN:
Gods! Free me from these labors!
I've spent a whole year up here, watching,
propped up on my elbows, on the roof
of this house of Atreus, like some dog.
How well I've come to know night's congregation of stars,   5
the blazing monarchs of the sky, those that bring winter
and those that bring summer to us mortals.
I know just when they rise and when they set.
So I watch, watch for the signal pyre,
the burning flame that will tell us, Troy is taken!

I take my orders from a woman, my mistress who waits for
    news,   10
oh she's a woman all right, a woman with a man's heart.
So I lie here, tossing and turning all night,

Opening: The appearance of the watchman may have been the first
time the roof of a scene building was used for the entrance of a character on the Athenian stage.

4: Atreus, the previous ruler of Argos, was the father of Agamemnon
and Menelaus.

this sopping bed unvisited by dreams.
Fear sits by my side and keeps me awake,
15 oh, I wish I could just close my eyes up tight ... and sleep.
So I sing to myself or hum a little tune,
a musical remedy, in case I drop off.
But it always makes me miserable and I start to cry,
for this house and how things used to be run, in the old days.
But if only tonight could come blessed freedom from these
20   labors.
Oh, let the fire of fortune light up our darkness.

(He sees the beacon shining in the distance.)

Oh! Oh! Welcome, beacon of the night, bright as day!
They'll be dancing all over Argos,
rejoicing this moment,
25 Yes! Yes!

I'm shouting to wake the wife of Agamemnon,
she must rise up out of bed, quickly, wake the house
and welcome this signal fire with the hallowed cry.
If Troy has been taken, as these flames
30 tell me, then I'll be the first
to sing and dance in celebration.
My master's luck is mine, this blazing
torch has thrown triple sixes for me!

Just bring my King home and let me clasp
35 his most welcome hand in mine. As for the rest,
I'm saying nothing, a great ox is standing on my tongue.
Now if this house could speak it would tell quite a story,
I've only got words for those in the know,
for the others, I can't remember anything.

(Exit watchman from the roof)

39: The chorus enters from the *eisodoi* (wings) into the orchestra. We
cannot know from the text from which direction they entered or even if
they came on from both sides. This edition assigns the wing entrances
here based on stage right for characters coming from Argos and stage
left for those arriving from elsewhere.

*(Enter the chorus of twelve Argive elders from the stage right
wing into the orchestra)*

CHORUS:
It has been ten years since
the great prosecutor of Priam,   40
Menelaus, and King Agamemnon,
the sons of Atreus,
twinned in throne and scepter
and yoked together by Zeus-given power,
launched from this land   45
a thousand Argive ships,
a force to vindicate our honor.
From their hearts they screamed a mighty cry
to the god of war. Like vultures grieving wildly
for stolen young kidnapped from their lofty nests,   50
whirling round and round, churning
the air with the oar-blades of their wings.
All their protective care made futile,
the young are lost forever.
Yet, above is one—Apollo, Pan or Zeus,   55
who hears the anguished cries
of these sky-borne guests,
and hurls on the guilty ones,
the wrath of a vengeful Fury!

40: King of Troy, the father of fifty children including Paris, Hector, and Cassandra.

41: Menelaus was the ruler of Sparta, brother of Agamemnon and the husband of Helen.

44: The highest of all the Olympian gods and primary arbiter of justice.

55: Apollo was the son of Zeus and a god associated with many functions including healing, prophecy, and music. He also hears the Paean, the ritual song delivered to gain the support of the gods. Pan was depicted as half man/half goat and was worshipped as a spirit of rustic pursuits. Pan's military function involves protecting soldiers in frontier regions and causing panic to descend on the enemy.

59: The *Erinyes* (Furies) were female underworld spirits that avenged familial bloodshed, protected the sanctity of sacred oaths, and restored the natural order.

60   *Zeus, the god of guests, drove*
          Atreus' proud sons at Paris,
          all for a woman bedded by many,
          a generation brought to their knees,
          wrestled down, ground into dust,
65   *Greek and Trojan spears shatter*
          in the marriage rites of blood.
          It is the way of Destiny
          that what will be, will be,
          and neither by burning offerings on high,
70   *nor pouring sacred wine below,*
          can you calm the relentless rage.
          We are the men without honor,
          our aging limbs incapable of service,
          left behind, propped on sticks,
75   *our brittle bones*
          as weak as children's.
          Unfit to serve the god of war,
          our bodies withering,
          in the autumn of our years.
80   *We go our three-footed way,*
          capable of no more than a child,
          wandering like a dream in the daylight.

        (The chorus addresses the house.)

       But you! Tyndareos' daughter,
       Queen Clytemnestra,

61: A Trojan prince, son of Priam and Hecuba who caused the Trojan War by abducting Helen from Sparta.

67: Destiny or "Fate" has the sense of "share" or "appointed lot" and is described throughout the trilogy in several ways; as a natural force, a presiding deity, a collection of female spirits ("the fates") who weave one's destiny and in terms of a final inevitable death.

84: The previous ruler of Sparta, husband of Leda, and father to Helen, Clytemnestra, and the Dioscuri. He made all the suitors of Helen promise to uphold her marriage to Menelaus. Some editions of the play place her actual entrance here.

85: Daughter of Tyndareos and Leda, sister of Helen, and wife of Agamemnon.

what is happening? What news? 85
What have you heard?
What message has persuaded you
to order sacrifices throughout the city?
All the gods that rule the city,
those above and those below, 90
gods of the gates, gods of the market.
All their altars blaze with offerings.
Everywhere the torches reach up
high into the flaming sky,
coaxed by soothing sacred oils 95
and pure lavish ointments,
offerings from the chambers of the Queen.
Tell us what you know, if you can, if it's right,
cure the foreboding that throbs in our heads.
Our thoughts are full of evil 100
that tears our hearts and burns in the brain,
yet these sacrifices ignite our hopes.
Heal our fear-infected minds!

[Strophe 1]

I can speak of the omen given to those mighty men
before they took ship, divine Persuasion breathes 105
through my song, the strength that grows with life.
I can tell how the twin-throned power of the Greeks
joint rulers of the youth of Hellas, 110
received a sign from the furious eagles
and hurled against Troy the spear of war!
The kings of the birds for the kings of the ships,
one black, the other white-tailed, appeared 115
on the lucky spear-arm side of the palace.
They perched there clutching a pregnant hare
who never had the chance for one last run,
and in full view feasted on her unborn young. 120

Cry, cry the song of sorrow, but let the good prevail.

105: *Peitho* ("Persuasion") was a minor female deity and the spirit of subtle and often sexual influence.

110: The name used by the Greeks to define their homeland.

[Antistrophe 1]

The army's trusted prophet saw how the two warrior sons
of Atreus, the commanders of the fleet, resembled
125   the hare-devouring eagles. He made this prophecy:
"One day this invading army will seize
Priam's city, but not before its herds
have bled away beneath the towers,
130   doomed to Destiny's death.
But let no envious god cast a cloud of darkness
over this mighty force that will harness Troy.
Beware, for Artemis, pure goddess, feels pity.
135   She resents her father's winged hounds
for the sacrifice of the trembling creature,
the parent's own young. She hates the eagle's feast.

Cry, cry the song of sorrow, but let the good prevail.

[Epode]

140   Beautiful Artemis kind even
to the fiercest lion's cub,
she takes delight in the suckling young
of all wild beasts that roam the fields.
She begs to fulfill these signs,
145   for the omen I saw was both good and evil.
I call on Apollo, god of healing:
Calm her, let her not send savage storms
to keep the Greeks from sailing,
demanding another sacrifice,
150   unspeakable, uneatable,
crafting ingrained, inborn strife.
Fearless of any man it waits,
this recurring, persistent terror,
the covert keeper of the House,
155   unforgiving child-avenging Rage!"

134: The daughter of Zeus and Leto. Goddess of the hunt, particularly
associated with female rites of passage such as marriage, childbirth,
and the rearing of young.

155: This is *Menis*, the personification of the spirit of divine wrath.

This was the prophecy shrieked
by Calchas to the royal House,
signs of great good and portents of doom,
and we sing the same bittersweet harmony.

Cry, cry the song of sorrow, but let the good prevail.

[Strophe 2]

Zeus, whoever you may be,   160
whatever name should please you,
I call to you!
When all things are weighed,
there is nothing else, only Zeus,
if I am to lift this futile burden   165
and ease my anxious mind.

[Antistrophe 2]

Once Ouranus swelling with pride
and insolence, held heaven's power,
he is nothing now, gone, forgotten.   170
Cronus, his successor, met his match,
downed on the third fall, overthrown!
Any man who shouts his victory-song to Zeus
will hit the mind's mark of true understanding.   175

[Strophe 3]

He set us mortals on the road to understanding,
and he has laid down his law:
"Man must learn by suffering!"
Not even sleep can relieve the painful memories
that fall upon the heart, drop by drop,   180
discretion comes even to the unwilling.

157: Calchas was the prophet of the Greek army at Troy.

168: The son and then husband of Gaia (Earth). He was the original sky father, usurped by his son, Cronus.

171: The son of Ouranus and Gaia. He married his sister Rhea and produced the Olympian gods. He was overthrown by his offspring, led by Zeus.

This grace is forced upon us
by sacred spirits who reign above.

[Antistrophe 3]

And on that day the First Sea Lord
185   *of the Greek ships*
did not blame any prophets,
he swayed with the winds of fortune.
The Greek force was unable to sail,
and they started to suffer and starve,
190   *sitting in their ships, off the coast of Chalcis,*
rocked back and forth, by the swelling tides of Aulis.

[Strophe 4]

Bitter winds blew down from the Strymon,
bringing hunger and delay to that wretched harbor,
driving the men to wander on the edge of insanity,
195   *wearing thin the cables and rotting the ships.*
Time, crawling slowly by, wore them down
the flower of Greek manhood
began to wither and waste away.
Then the prophet cried out,
200   *in the name of Artemis,*
proclaiming a remedy to soothe the storm,
and the sons of Atreus
beat the ground with their scepters,
unable to hold back a flood of tears.

[Antistrophe 4]

205   *Then Agamemnon, the eldest, spoke:*
"An unbearable fate will fall on me if I disobey

190: The main city of Euboea in the Eastern part of Greece. Its name means "Coppertown."

191: Aulis lies on the Boeotian coast directly across the straits of Euripos from Chalcis. This was the place where the Greek fleet gathered before sailing on Troy.

192: A river in Thrace to the north of Greece.

but how can I bear to slaughter my own daughter,
the glory of my House?
How can I stain my hands, the hands of a father,
with this young girl's blood, as it drenches the altar? 210
How can I choose? Both ways are full of evil!
Should I desert the fleet and fail my allies?
The sacrifice stops the storm,
the blood of a virgin must be spilled,
rage craves rage, 215
what must be must be.
Let it be for the best."

[Strophe 5]

And as he strapped himself to the yoke of Necessity,
his storm-swept psyche veered on an impious course,
impure, unholy, unsanctified. 220
At that very moment he changed
and his altered mind would dare do anything.
Such shameless thoughts make mere men bold,
maddening minds and reducing them to ruin.
And so he dared to sacrifice his daughter, 225
a first offering to bless the fleet,
to fight that woman-revenging war.

[Antistrophe 5]

Her pleading, her terrified cries of "Father!"
her pure young life, counted for nothing
with the chiefs, they were too hungry for war. 230
Her father prayed to the gods, then ordered
his men to raise her up over the altar,
face down, like some sacrificial goat.
She fell at his feet, clasping his robes,
begging for mercy with heart-rending cries. 235
He ordered her beautiful mouth to be gagged,
to stifle a cry that would curse the House.

218: This is *Ananke*, the personification of compulsive force.

[Strophe 6]

And as the bridle forced her silence,
steeped saffron poured to the ground.
240 *Her eyes threw a last pitiful glance at her sacrificers,*
but like a figure in a painting,
she could not call to them for help.
How often she had sung to these same men
as guests in her father's House,
245 *how many times her pure young voice*
had so lovingly sung, for her father,
the sacred song at the third libation.

[Antistrophe 6]

What happened next, I did not see and I cannot tell,
but the prophecies of Calchas are always fulfilled.
250 *Justice will tip the scales,*
to bring learning through suffering.
You will know the future when it comes, until then let it be,
to know the future is to bring sorrow in advance,
it will all come clear in the light of dawn
255 *and let all that comes now turn out for the best.*

(Enter Clytemnestra from the doorway)

As is surely the wish of our guardian here,
the sole sentinel of Argos, the bulwark of our land.

(The chorus addresses Clytemnestra.)

I have come, Clytemnestra, respectful of your power,
it is just to honor the wife of a ruler
260 when her husband's throne is vacant.

239: "Steeped saffron" may refer to Iphigenia's dyed yellow wedding
veil or dress. The unveiling of a bride before her groom was an important part of an Athenian marriage ceremony. Saffron is also used as a
description for blood at line 1121. Here Aeschylus depicts a shocking
corruption of a marriage ceremony.

247: At a banquet guests poured three offerings of wine: the first to the
Olympian gods, the second to the heroes, and the third to Zeus.

250: This is *Dike*, the daughter of Zeus and *Themis* ("Right"), the personification of justice.

Have you heard some good news, some new hope?
Is this why you are making these sacrifices?
We would be grateful to hear, but will respect your silence.

CLYTEMNESTRA:
Good news. As the proverb says:
"May morning born of Mother Night, bring tidings of joy!"   265
I have great news to tell you, beyond all your hopes.
The Greeks have captured Priam's city!

CHORUS:
What? I don't understand. I can't believe what you are saying.

CLYTEMNESTRA:
The Greeks have taken Troy! Is that clear enough for you?

CHORUS:
I'm so happy I could cry.   270

CLYTEMNESTRA:
Your eyes proclaim your loyalty.

CHORUS:
Are you convinced? Do you have proof?

CLYTEMNESTRA:
Of course. Unless a god deceives me with a trick.

CHORUS:
So you believe in the persuasive power of dreams.

CLYTEMNESTRA:
I do not accept guidance from a mind asleep.   275

258ff: It must be remembered that the actors performed in masks, and
thus that all dialogue had to be performed on a "split focus" (both actors
facing the front though addressing each other). A mask turned upstage
would fail to engage the audience and would probably not be audible.

265: This saying is not found elsewhere but has sinister connotations.
The personification of Night was *Nyx*, daughter of Chaos and mother
to the Furies and Strife.

CHORUS:
Perhaps you have heard a rumor then, and it has kindled
    your hopes?

CLYTEMNESTRA:
Don't insult my intelligence. You treat me like a child.

CHORUS:
But when was the city captured?

CLYTEMNESTRA:
During the night, which has now given birth to this dawning
    light.

CHORUS:
280   What messenger could possibly reach here so quickly?

CLYTEMNESTRA:
Hephaestus sent his brilliant courier from Mount Ida,
and from beacon to beacon the signal flame flashed here.
From Ida to the rock of Hermes at Lemnos,
from that island, third in line, on to Mount Athos,
285   sacred to Zeus, the great flame blazed.
Then, onward and upward, gaining strength,
soaring high above the seas,
this mighty torch forged ahead.
Sunlike, the pine-wood fires passed

281: Hephaestus was the god of fire, the forge, smiths, and craftsmen.
Mt. Ida is the peak that overlooks the plain of Troy and site of the judgment of Paris.

283: Hermes was the messenger of the gods and escort to the dead.
Lemnos is an island in the northern Aegean off the coast of Asia Minor.
According to mythology the Lemnian women had all murdered their
husbands.

284: The mountain which stands on the eastern promontory of Chal-
cidice on the coast of Thrace. Its third position may be a reference to
Zeus Soter ("The Savior," also called Zeus the Third) in his guise as a
god or fulfiller of destiny.

their golden message to Macistus' tall towers. 290
Straightway, the vigilant watchman,
shaking off exhaustion, did his duty,
and far over Euripos' stream shone the beacon's light,
signaling to the sentinels on Messapion.
They, kindling a heap of brittle brushwood, 295
lit their answering fires and sent the message on.
Vaulting the plain of Asopus,
the never-dimming flame burned brighter still,
shining like the radiant moon,
until it reached the rocks of Cithaeron. 300
There, the watchful guards lit a blaze
brighter than they were ordered, and shot
the light far across Gorgopus' swamp,
to fall upon the heights of Aegiplanctus.
Without question or delay they built 305
a mighty beard of flame so vast it reached
even the Saronic gulf's jutting headland.
On it sped, down to the lookout near our city,
perched on the peak of Arachnaeus,
until, at last, it struck the roof of this House of Atreus, 310
a flame akin to its Trojan ancestor.
This relay-race of torches where all complete
the course and both first and last are victors,
was arranged at my command.

290: This is unknown, but it may have been a mountain in Euboea.

293: The body of water between Chalcis and Aulis and the site of the murder of Iphigenia, Agamemnon's daughter.

294: A mountain on the Boeotian coast.

297: A river in Boeotia.

300: The mountain range that borders Attica and Boeotia, the place where the infant Oedipus was exposed.

303: This means "Gorgon's swamp." The site is unknown, but its name is a reference to the female monsters that could turn a man to stone.

304: This location is also not known, but it means "goat-roaming peak."

307: The body of water between Attica and the Argolid.

309: This means "spider mountain" and has been identified as Mt. Arna to the north of Argos.

315   This is my proof, the sign I spoke of,
        my husband's message, sent from Troy.

CHORUS:
        My lady, I shall offer thanks to the gods.
        But, please tell us everything again,
        I can only marvel at your words.

CLYTEMNESTRA:
320   Today the Greeks hold Troy,
        its streets echo to the harsh cries of discordant voices.
        Pour vinegar and oil into the same jar
        and like enemies they will separate,
        just like the cries of victors and vanquished,
325   distinct as their different fortunes.
        Cries, howled over the corpses of husbands,
        brothers, children, and fathers.
        A lamenting wail from throats enslaved
        mourning the death of loved ones, the loss of life.
330   For the victors, after the battle,
        a night spent scavenging
        through the Trojan streets,
        hungrily breakfasting on the city's scraps,
        as chance not rank dictates.
335   Now they rest in captured Trojan homes,
        free from the frost and damp of the open sky,
        lucky men, a sound night's sleep, at last unguarded.
        Now, if only they respect the captured city's gods
        and honor their holy places,
340   the victors will not be vanquished.
        Let no unbridled lust run riot through our army,
        overpowered by greed to snatch forbidden fruits.
        To win safe passage home they must turn back down
        the final stretch and complete the course.
345   Even if the army returns safely, without transgressing
        heaven, the malice of the dead might yet be stirred
        and bring about some sudden act of evil.
        You have heard my words, women's words,
        be in no doubt, we will see good prevail,
350   this would bring me joy above all other blessings.

CHORUS:
  Lady, you speak wisely like a man of discretion,
  and now that I have heard your proof

  (Exit Clytemnestra through the doorway)

  I will prepare to offer prayers to the gods,
  such an outcome deserves my gratitude.

[Prelude]

Zeus great king, and you kind Night,   355
resplendent in your brilliant glories,
you flung that dark mesh,
your vast enslaving net,
enveloping Troy's ramparts,
trawling young and old   360
to all-embracing Ruin.
Great Zeus, god of guests, I honor you,
you have done this! All that time
stretching your bow against Paris,
your deadly arrow never fell short,   365
nor flew, wasted, beyond the stars.

[Strophe 1]

The Trojans can tell how it feels to be struck
by the hand of Zeus, the course was clear
and he has done what he decreed.
The one who says that gods pay no heed   370
to mortals who trample sacred grace,
holds heaven in contempt.
A curse will appear to the future generations
of those who dare such insolence.   375
Those who set themselves beyond Justice,
cramming their homes with riches,
overstep the bounds of what is best.

361: This is *Ate*, the personification of ruin and a force of mental delusion that causes ultimate disaster.

Let each man have enough, no more,
380   *let him know the limit of his needs,*
then we might avoid this suffering.
There can be no defense for the man
who gorges himself with the fat of wealth,
and kicks the altar of Justice far from sight.

[Antistrophe 1]

385   *The wretched spirit of Persuasion,*
conniving child of Ruin, forces him on,
remedy is futile, the crime cannot be hidden,
like a beacon's blaze the evil shines out.
390   *The grinding stone scratches the surface,*
the metal of the man turns true,
bad bronze blackened and base.
Like a child chasing a bird in flight,
Justice eludes him, and he taints
395   *his city with the touch of terror.*
All the gods are deaf to his prayers,
for transgressors are pulled down
and the unjust are destroyed.
Such a man was Paris, who came
400   *as a guest to the House of Atreus*
and shamed all hospitality
by stealing another man's wife.

[Strophe 2]

For us, her people, she left behind the din
of clashing shields and spears,
405   *as the war fleets armed.*
Taking with her a dowry of destruction,
she strode swiftly through that city's gates,
daring what must not be dared.
Then the prophets of this House cried out:
410   *"Oh the House, the House and its masters!*
Oh the marriage bed, where love once lay!"
Now there is only the lonely anguish of a man,
dishonored, but too stunned to blame.
Now a ghostly figure walks in his House,
415   *as he longs for the woman far across the sea.*

He turns with hatred from statues
carved to her grace and beauty,
her eyes gaze out, empty and cold,
their love has faded, its power has gone.

[Antistrophe 2]

In his grief-stricken dreams 420
he sees her, joy and pain.
He reaches out to touch,
but her figure slips through
his desperate arms
and is gone, lost forever, 425
drifting on the wings of sleep.
Such are the sorrows of this House,
and worse, sorrows spread
through all the homes of Greece,
left empty of their men. 430
Women sound the sorrows,
sorrows that tear at the heart.
Men we all knew,
sent out to war,
returning home, 435
ashes in urns.

[Strophe 3]

Ares, god of war, dealer in death,
holds the scales in the battle of spears.
He returns from Troy in exchange for men, 440
the heavy dust, purified in the fire,
washed by the tears of loved ones.
He stows the ships with an easy cargo,
ashes crammed into urns.
So they lament, honoring each man in turn: 445
"How skilled he was in battle,"
or: "How bravely he fell in combat"
"All for another man's wife!"
Is whispered in secret.

438: The son of Zeus and Hera and the god of war and destruction.

450   *Resentment, fueled by grief, spreads stealthily*
       against the sons of Atreus, defenders of Justice.
       Around the walls of Troy young men,
       cut down in their prime,
       lie buried in the land
455   *they came to conquer.*

[Antistrophe 3]

       I can hear the dangerous murmur
       of angry citizens, it is the people's curse,
       the penalty that must be paid.
460   *There is something hidden in the darkness.*
       The gods are not blind
       to men who bring slaughter,
       the dark Furies will pull down
       the man who unjustly prospers,
465   *reversing his fortunes, grinding*
       him down. A shadow, beyond all help.
       He is lost forever.
       High ambition is fraught with peril,
       for Zeus sees all and hurls
470   *his fiery thunderbolt.*
       Give me good fortune without envy
       I've no wish to plunder cities,
       but I'll not waste my life away
       as another man's slave.

[Epode]

475   *Fire, bringing good news,*
       flashes through the city,
       igniting rumors—is it true? Who knows?
       Perhaps the gods are deceiving us.

       Who is so childish and senseless
480   *as to let some burning signal*

471: "Good fortune" is *olbos*, the concept of happiness, prosperity, and
contentment.

fire up their heart with hope, only
to be dashed when the real word comes.

Trust a woman to praise a sign
before the truth is clear.
Persuasion is all too quick   485
to cross a woman's mind.
Women's gossip flies fast and quickly dies.

We will soon find out about this relay
of flaming torches, we will know whether   490
they are true, or whether like a dream
this happy light has beguiled our brains.

(The chorus spots a herald coming in the distance.)

But look there! I can see a herald from the shore,
his head is shaded with olive branches.
Our witness covered in mud and dust,   495
not some speechless pile of blazing mountain
wood sending smoke signals from a fire.
He will speak with a real voice and bring us
great news, great joy, or else ... no, not that.
Good is coming! Bring on the good news!   500
And if anyone here does not pray for this,
let them reap the harvest of a sick mind.

(Enter herald from the stage left wing)

HERALD:
Oh, land of my ancestors! Good Greek soil!
Back at last after ten long years away,
all my hopes cut away, except one,   505
I never dreamed I would be buried in my own land,
in Argive soil, where I belong.
Welcome native earth, welcome light of the sun.
I give thanks to almighty Zeus, and to you,
Pythian Apollo, shoot no more arrows at us,   510

494: The messenger's wreath indicates that he is bearing good news.

510: This is a cult title of Apollo in his guise as presider over the oracle
at Delphi.

you were fierce enough at Scamander's banks,
but now, be our savior and our healer.
I salute Lord Apollo and all the gods of the city,
especially my guardian, the loving herald,
515   Hermes, sacred to all messengers.
I salute our patron heroes who sent us on our way,
welcome home the remnants of our army,
those of us who escaped the spear.
Halls of kings, beloved chambers, sacred thrones,
520   sun-facing spirits, who used to greet him with glad eyes,
after all these years receive again your master.
He comes bringing light in the darkness,
for one and for all ... King Agamemnon!
Give him the welcome he deserves.
525   The man who brought the justice of Zeus down
on Troy like a mighty pickaxe smashing her to rubble.
The altars and shrines to her gods have been destroyed
and her seed of life ground into the dust.
Such was the yoke of slavery he threw on Troy.
530   Our king, eldest son of Atreus, the most blessed,
and worthy man alive, is coming.
Neither Paris, nor the city that shared his guilt,
can boast the crime exceeded the punishment.
Convicted of rape and theft, he has lost his precious
535   plunder and brought utter destruction on his city.
His father's House and his homeland laid waste.
Twice over, the sons of Priam have paid for their crimes.

CHORUS:
Welcome home, messenger of the Greek armies.

HERALD:
It's good to be home. Now I could die happy if the gods
willed it.

511: A river on the Trojan plain now called the Menderes su.

520: A possible reference to the representations of household gods or
Argive heroes that are imagined to stand on or by the House of Atreus.

CHORUS:
  Did you feel such pain being away from your country? 540

HERALD:
  Yes, but now I could cry with happiness.

CHORUS:
  At least there is some joy in your pain.

HERALD:
  What do you mean? I don't understand, tell me.

CHORUS:
  You yearned for those who yearned for you.

HERALD:
  While we missed home, you missed the army? 545

CHORUS:
  So much that our minds filled with sick shadows.

HERALD:
  But why were you so anxious for the return of the army?

CHORUS:
  For a long time now silence has kept me free from harm.

HERALD:
  What? Have you been living in fear while your leaders have
    been away?

CHORUS:
  As you said, now would be a good time to die. 550

HERALD:
  Yes, we did what we set out to do,
  it took a long time, but we did it.
  Some things turned out well, others went badly.
  Who in this life, save a god, is free from suffering?
  You wouldn't believe what we had to put up with, 555
  crammed into ships, jammed in narrow gangways,

berthed on bare boards, hardship every single day.
Then, ashore, it was even worse,
camped under the enemy walls, constantly
560   soaked to the skin with damp and drizzle,
our clothes rotting, and our hair crawling with lice.
Then there was the winter's cold, the snows from Mount Ida
that froze even the birds to death. Too cold to bear!
And the heat, the breathless windless noons,
565   the waveless waters, sun-stunned to a dead calm.
But why complain now? Our work is done
and the dead can finally rest.
Why count the cost? We, the living,
can't complain about the hand of fortune,
570   good riddance to all our troubles.
For us, the remnants of the Argive army,
we've been lucky, the scales have come down
in our favor, we've won the right to shout
our proud boast in the light of the sun,
575   and spread our fame over land and sea;
"Once an Argive-led army conquered Troy
and hung their spoils in every temple,
throughout all of Greece, proof of past glories."
When they hear this, men will respect this city,
580   praise our commanders, and honor Zeus,
this was his doing, give thanks to him!
I have told you what I had to say, you have heard the news.

CHORUS:
Your words have convinced me and proved me wrong,
men are never too old to learn. This news should
585   be told to Clytemnestra and the household,
but I feel a richer man for having heard it.

(Enter Clytemnestra from the doors)

CLYTEMNESTRA:
I cried out for joy long before this,
when the first burning messenger came by night,
590   telling me of Troy's capture and destruction.
Then there were those that criticized me,
saying, "A few beacons convince you that Troy is taken,

isn't that just like a woman to be led by her heart,"
implying that I had lost my wits.
But I continued with my woman's sacrifices
and all over the city the hallowed cry rang out,   595
and in the holy shrines of our gods, the fire
was lulled by the sweet-smelling incense.

There is no need for you to tell me any more,
I shall learn the whole story from the king himself.
Now I must prepare the best welcome a man can have,   600
there is no day's dawning light happier
for a woman as when she unbars the door
to her man, back from war, spared by the gods.
Tell my husband all this and tell him to come
as quickly as possible, the city's darling.   605
Let him find a faithful wife in his home,
just as he left her, the watchdog of his house,
loyal only to him, an enemy to his enemies.
I have not changed. In all this time
I've kept our promises, never broken our seal.   610
There has been no scandal, I know as much about
the pleasures of another man as I do of steeping metal.
This is my boast, and it is true,
it would not disgrace the noblest of women.

(Exit Clytemnestra through the doors)

CHORUS:
So she says, but you need no prophet   615
to interpret these seemingly good words.
Tell me, Herald, what about Menelaus,
our land's beloved lord, has he returned home
safely from his voyage? Is he with you?

612: This intriguing phrase initially seems to be a colloquialism for a
lack of knowledge of male crafts ("I know as much about infidelity as I
do of metal working"). However, "steeping metal" also suggests the
impending murder of Agamemnon. It may well be a reference to the
death of Iphigenia. The word "steeped" was used in this context at line
239 (see note) and the Greek word for metal (*chalcous*) would remind
the audience of Chalcis, where her sacrifice occurred.

HERALD:
620   I couldn't lie to you, my friend,
       your happiness would be short lived.

CHORUS:
       If only you could bring us news that is both true and good,
       but you can't hide the real truth from us.

HERALD:
       Then I'll tell you the truth: both the man
625   and his ship vanished from our sight.

CHORUS:
       Did you see him set sail from Troy, or did a storm
       scatter you all and snatch him from the fleet?

HERALD:
       You've hit the mark, just like a skillful bowman,
       in a few short words you've said it all.

CHORUS:
630   What are the other crews saying?
       Is he alive or dead?

HERALD:
       Nobody knows and none can say,
       except perhaps Helios, the sun god.

CHORUS:
       Tell me how the storm struck, how did it end?
635   Was it sent by vengeful spirits?

HERALD:
       It is wrong to defile a day of good news with dark words,
       the honored gods keep such things apart.
       When a messenger comes to his people bringing
       the disastrous news of their army's destruction,
640   the war god wields his double scourge.

633: Perceived as a charioteer who rode his sun chariot from east to west,
Helios was said to be able to see the entire world on his journey.

One crack of the lash stings the whole city,
but from every home Ares claims his victims,
double-edged destruction, a bloody partnership.
A messenger bearing such dreadful news
can at least invoke the Furies,   645
but when he delivers news of salvation
to a city celebrating her success,
how can I mix good with bad and tell you?
Tell you about the storm sent by the angry gods.

Those great old enemies, Fire and Water,   650
swore an alliance and wrecked the Greek fleet.
That night a vast, cruel swell rose up,
followed by the howling winds blasting
down from Thrace. Ship was sent crashing
into ship, and the sheets of rain   655
and fierce gales swept our fleet from sight,
like sheep sent reeling by some evil shepherd.
When the sun rose, bringing light,
we saw the Aegean sea blossom.
With corpses and shattered wrecks.   660
But for us, our ship was untouched,
someone, something, not human,
stole us away and took up our helm,
luck boarded our vessel and saved us.
We rode out the waves at anchor   665
and were kept well away from the rocky coast.
We couldn't believe our fortune on that bright day,
we had escaped a watery grave.
And then it dawned on us,
the fleet scattered and wrecked,   670
if any of the crews were still drawing breath,
they would be thinking that we were lost,
and why not? We thought the same of them.
And Menelaus, he'll be back, I'm sure of it,
if he is still out there, somewhere under the sun,   675
he will survive, if it is the plan of Zeus.
I know it will all turn out for the best,

654: Thrace was the colder, mountainous region to the north of Greece.
The bitter northern winds were said to originate there.

Zeus will not destroy this family,
there is still hope that he will return.
680   Now you have it, I have told you the truth.

(Exit herald through the stage left wing)

[Strophe 1]

CHORUS:
Who was it who gave her
such a fitting name?
Did some invisible power
guide his tongue,
685   *knowing what Destiny held in store?*
A bride of the spear, a strife-bringer,
Helen! She lived up to her name,
and no mistake, hell to ships!
690   *Hell to men! Hell to the city!*
As she dipped her delicate veil,
and sailed away, wafted
on Zephyrus' passionate breath.
695   *Many warrior hunters followed*
in the tracks of the vanished oar-wash,
now beached on Simois' leafy shores.
Oars that stroked the blood of Strife.

[Antistrophe 1]

Rage bought a marriage of mourning,
700   *rightly named, to Troy and fulfilled*
the dishonor to a hospitable hearth,
and dishonor to Zeus, god of guests.
Vengeance fell on the House of the groom,
705   *those who sang so loud the wedding song,*
honoring the bride with festive hymns,
have had to learn a different tune.

694: The west wind.

697: A river on the plain of Troy.

698: This is *Eris*, the spirit of discord and a daughter of Night. She created the rivalry between the goddesses that led to the judgment of Paris and in turn the Trojan War.

Now Priam's ancient city
moans the melody of mourning,
bitter laments that name Paris   710
as the man who wedded evil.
The city swells with so much sorrow,
and the death wails drone the doom   715
for a slaughtered people, for the pain of death.

[Strophe 2]

Once a man reared in his House,
a lion cub, torn from the breast
while still a suckling whelp.
When little it was so gentle   720
and friendly to children,
and always a delight to the old.
He would cradle it in his arms,
like a newborn, bright-eyed baby,
feeding it from his own hand   725
whenever it was hungry.

[Antistrophe 2]

But as time passed it showed
the true temper of its breed
and returned its foster parents'
kindness by slaughtering their herds.   730
A foul forbidden feast that stained
the house with the stench of blood.
This pain that none could fight
wreaked havoc in the House,
for they had raised, within their home,   735
A god-sent priest of Ruin.

[Strophe 3]

I imagine what first came to Troy
resembled a spirit of windless calm,
a delicate ornament of luxury,   740
seductive glances darting from the eyes,
and passion blossoming in the hearts of men.
But then she veered her course
and brought a bitter end to this marriage,

745   *for Zeus, the god of guests,*
        sent an evil escort
        to the children of Priam,
        one that brings tears to brides:
        the Fury!

[Antistrophe 3]

750   *There is a time-honored saying,*
        that a man's good fortune at its height
        does not die without giving birth.
        For happiness always
755   *cultivates insatiable misery,*
        to curse the future generations.
        But I believe something different;
        it is the evil deed itself
        that spawns further evil,
760   *the very image of the breed.*
        Beautiful children will always bless
        The House of the just and good.

[Strophe 4]

     Outrage of old longs
        to breed in evil people.
765   *Sooner or later the time comes*
        and it will be born again,
        the ever-hungry spirit,
        unconquerable, invincible,
        unsanctified and insolent,
770   *blackening the halls with Ruin,*
        a child in the mold of its parents.

[Antistrophe 4]

     Justice shines her light
        on humble, smoke-filled homes,
775   *honoring the righteous man.*
        The gold-encrusted palaces
        where the hands of men are tainted,
        she abandons with eyes averted.
        She has no respect for the power of wealth,

stamped with the false mark of men's approval,   780
for in the end it is she who divides the share.*

> (Enter Agamemnon and Cassandra in a chariot from the stage
> left wing into the orchestra)

Come then, King, conqueror of Troy,
son of Atreus.
How should I salute you?
How to honor you correctly,   785
neither exceeding the limit
nor falling short of due homage?
Many men praise appearances
and overstep the bounds of Justice.
Anyone can say they share the grief   790
of the unfortunate, but the stab of pain
will never twist in their hearts.
Some pretend to share in a man's glory,
forcing their faces into a smile,
but the good shepherd, who knows his flock,   795
is not fooled by eyes that lie,
feigning a loyal disposition
and fawning with tearful affection.
When you were gathering the armies
for the sake of Helen, my mind painted   800
an ugly picture of you, I don't deny it.
I thought you must have lost all grip
on your senses, when you dared
that sacrifice, to save your dying men.
But now, from a heart loyal and true I say: 805
"Well done to all who wrought this joyful end."
You will soon find out for yourself
which of your citizens, who stayed at home,
were just, and which abused your absence.

782: Agamemnon is more than likely unaccompanied by a guard. He
has come "as quickly as possible" (605), and the lack of a retinue makes
him visually vulnerable for the scene ahead.

AGAMEMNON:

810   First, it is right that I address Argos and the gods
         of this land—my allies who helped me exact
         justice from Priam's city and return home safely.
         The gods heard the case, it needed no words,
         they cast their votes into the urn of blood,
815   unanimously calling for the destruction of Troy
         and death for her men. Hope's hand hovered
         over the urn of pity, and left it empty.
         You can still see the smoke from the sacked city,
         the storm-winds of ruin are alive! And as the embers die,
820   the ashes of Troy's wealth are scattered to the wind.
         For this we must praise the gods with eternal gratitude.
         For their rape of a wife we exacted payment,
         for a woman, the beast of Argos
         ground their city to dust.
825   The deadly brood of the wooden horse,
         our shield wielding warriors,
         struck by night as the Pleiades set,
         and the battle-hungry lion leapt over the walls
         and feasted on the blood of kings!

830   This lengthy prelude I dedicate to the gods.
         Now to your concerns, I have not forgotten,
         I agree with you, and give you my support.
         There are not many who can admire a man
         for his success and not feel envy.
835   Envy eats away at a man's heart,
         a sickness that deals a double blow,
         for he buckles under the weight of his own grief
         and groans at the sight of another's good fortune.
         I speak from experience, how well I know
840   the flattering mirror of comradeship.
         They seemed so loyal once, shadows of real men!
         Only Odysseus, who sailed with me against his will,

827: This constellation is a group of seven stars that sets over Greece in
late autumn. This also signified the start of rough weather at sea.

842: Odysseus, Homer's great wandering hero and the ruler of Ithaca,
attempted to feign insanity before the Greek commanders in order to
avoid his conscription into the Trojan War.

proved a steady team-horse once yoked to me,
even as I speak, I do not know if he is alive or dead.

But now to matters of state and religion.   845
We must meet in council and call an assembly,
we will decide what is healthy and help it prosper,
but the sickness in the state must be cut away,
and burned clean to stem the spread of infection.
Now I will enter my house, my home,   850
and at the household hearth offer my first greeting
to the gods, they sent me, and they have brought me back.
Victory, you have been my constant companion,
may you stand by my side forever.

    (Enter Clytemnestra from the doors)

CLYTEMNESTRA:
Men of the city, elders of Argos,   855
I feel no shame in telling you of my love
for the man, shyness dies when one
gets older. I will speak from the heart,
I will tell you how unbearable my life has been
while this man stood under Troy's walls.   860
To begin with, when a woman sits at home,
parted from her husband, her loneliness is terrible,
and the rumors she hears spread like a disease.
A messenger comes to the house bringing bad news,
then another and the reports grow worse.   865
If this man had been struck as often
as false rumors flowed into this house,
then he would have more holes in him than a net.
If he had been killed as many times as the stories said,
he should have had three bodies, a second Geryon,   870
and could boast of wearing a triple cloak of earth,
for every time I was told that he was dead and buried.
These rumors ate away at me, to the point
that I had to be released, against my will,
from the noose of suicide, more than once.   875
This is why our child, the seal of our pledge,

870: A triple-bodied monster killed by Heracles.

is not here, standing by my side as is right.
Do not worry, Orestes our son is safe in the care
880   of our loyal ally, Strophius of Phocis.
He warned me of the dangers you would face,
battling under the walls of Troy,
and of the anger of the people who might
have rebelled against the council.
885   It is human nature to kick a man when he is down.
It was justified, you know I speak the truth.
As for me, I once cried rivers of tears,
but I can't any more, I have no more tears.
I sat up night after night, waiting,
890   my eyes sore with weeping, straining to see
the beacon-fires that were never lit.
I would be woken, by the slightest of sounds,
from dreams, where I saw you suffer more
than my sleeping hours could bear.

895   I endured all this and now my mind is free from pain,
I welcome this man, the watchdog of the fold,
the steadfast broad-beam of the ship, the strong pillar
of the towering roof, the one true heir to his father,
the sight of land to shipwrecked sailors,
900   the first fine day after the storm,
a refreshing stream to a thirsty traveler,
the sweet savior of all our stress.
Is he not worthy of this praise? Envy keep away,
we have already endured enough misfortune.

905   Come now my love, step down from the chariot,
do not place your kingly foot on common ground,
this is the foot that stamped out Troy.
Women! I have told you what to do.

> (Enter servant women from the doors. They lay a path of
> crimson tapestries from the doorway to the foot of Agamem-
> non's chariot.)

880: Phocis was a region in central Greece to the south of Mt. Parnassus.

Strew the path of his feet with these fabrics,
quickly! Cover his way with crimson, let Justice   910
lead him into the home he never expected to see again.
I will arrange everything else, my mind never sleeps,
and with the help of the gods I will set things right.

AGAMEMNON:
Daughter of Leda, guardian of my house,
your speech was like my absence, too long.   915
You should not praise me this way,
such words should come from others.
Do not pamper me like a woman, nor grovel
with a gaping mouth as if I were some barbarian chieftain.
Do not bring Envy on me by strewing my path with cloths,
only the gods should be honored this way.   920
I am a mortal man and the thought of stepping
on these beautiful embroideries fills me with dread.
Give me the honors due to a man, not a god,
you do not need to add to my fame   925
with these foot-cloths and fine fabrics.
A mind free from evil is heaven's greatest gift,
and a happy man is one who ends his life
having attained the good fortune he so cherishes.
If I can hold to this in all things then I need never fear.   930

CLYTEMNESTRA:
Then trust your judgment and tell me this.

AGAMEMNON:
Don't worry, my judgment will never be corrupted.

CLYTEMNESTRA:
Would you have promised this to the gods in a moment of
    terror?

AGAMEMNON:
Yes, if a seer told me that it would be for the best.

CLYTEMNESTRA:
What do you think Priam would have done if he had won?   935

AGAMEMNON:
I think he would have walked on these embroideries.

CLYTEMNESTRA:
Then do not be ashamed of the disapproval of men.

AGAMEMNON:
The voice of the people carries enormous power.

CLYTEMNESTRA:
But the unenvied man is unenviable.

AGAMEMNON:
940   A woman should not be so fond of argument.

CLYTEMNESTRA:
It becomes the fortunate man to yield a victory.

AGAMEMNON:
You really want your victory in this contest?

CLYTEMNESTRA:
Be persuaded, you have the power, surrender of your own
    free will, to me.

AGAMEMNON:
Well, if you want this so much. Here, somebody help me off
with my boots.

(A servant removes Agamemnon's boots.)

945   Trusty slaves, they have served me well.
And as I tread on these lavish sea-red cloths,
let no god's envious glare strike me from afar.
I am ashamed to let my feet ruin the wealth
of this house and waste these expensive threads.
Enough!

*(Agamemnon steps down from his chariot and onto the
tapestries.)*

It is done.

(Indicating Cassandra)

Take this stranger into the house,   *950*
be kind to her. The god looks down with good will
on the conqueror who can be kind;
nobody bears the yoke of slavery freely.
I have brought this girl with me, my gift from the army,
the choicest flower, the pick of the prizes.   *955*
And now since I have surrendered to your pleas,
I will go into the halls of my house, treading on crimson
    cloths.

*(Agamemnon turns and walks along the tapestries toward the
doors.)*

CLYTEMNESTRA:
There is the sea, who will ever drain it dry?
It will always teem thick with crimson, rich as silver,
a regenerating ooze to steep our fabrics.   *960*
This house has plenty, my king,
thanks to the gods we have never known poverty.
I would have pledged to tread an endless path
of tapestries, if an oracle had ordained
that it would bring the life back to the house.   *965*
As long as the root survives, new leaves will return
to spread their shade against the searing dog-star.
So you have returned to your hearth and home

955: Cassandra was the daughter of King Priam and a prophetess of
Apollo. The practice of claiming noble female captives as war prizes led
to the initial dispute between Agamemnon and Achilles in Book 1 of
Homer's *Iliad*. She wears the garlands of a priestess and clutches a
small ritual staff.

959: The ultraexpensive crimson dye was obtained from the murex, a
tiny shellfish. Thousands of these would have been needed to stain
such a large amount of fabric.

967: This is Sirius, the bright star that brings the dog days of summer
with its fierce heat and threat of disease. The appearance of Sirius may
have been linked with cult practice surrounding sacrifices associated
with the pleading for the renewal of vegetation. These took place at the
time of the old and new year, which fell in midsummer.

970   heralding warmth in the winter, and when Zeus
        ripens the bitter virgin fruit, to make wine,
        the house is cooled, when the appointed man
        sweeps, once again, though the halls.

        (*Agamemnon enters the doors.*)

        Zeus! Zeus fulfiller! Fulfill my prayers!
        Complete your plans, once and for all!

        (*Exit women through the doors with the tapestries, followed
        by Clytemnestra*)

[Strophe 1]

CHORUS:
975   *Why does this terror keep hovering*
        in front of my prophetic heart?
        Why is my song so full of foreboding?
        I do not want to hear it!
980   *Lost confidence unseats good sense.*
        Why can't I dismiss this feeling
        as just another muddled dream?
        So much time has passed,
        the mooring cables of the ships
985   *that were cut and left,*
        when they sailed for Troy
        are now buried deep in the sand.

[Antistrophe 1]

        I have seen him come home myself,
        I witnessed it with my own eyes!
990   *But my soul still echoes with the drone*
        of the lyreless hymn, I have learned
        the Furies' dirge of death
        and lost all strength of hope.
995   *The truth twists in my guts,*
        my heart throbs with foreboding,
        my head spins at the thought
        of the fulfillment of Justice.
        I pray that my fears are groundless,
1000   *let them not be fulfilled.*

[Strophe 2]

Even good health can exceed its limits;
its neighbor, sickness, is always there,
there is only a small wall between them.
It is just the same with the fortunes of man,   1005
even when he holds a straight course,
he can still strike the unseen reef of disaster.
But if in advance, caution throws overboard
some of the cargo of his wealth,
creating a proper balance,   1010
then the whole House will not sink,
overwhelmed by its own abundance,
the hull of that ship will stay afloat.
Just as the generous gift of Zeus is harvested,   1015
each year, from the furrows of the land
holding back the disease of famine.

[Antistrophe 2]

But once the dark blood of a murdered
man has been spilt on the ground,   1020
what magic can bring it back?
Only Asclepius knew
how to raise the dead,
and Zeus punished him severely.
If only the gods had not ordained   1025
that our destinies clash
to keep us in check,
then my heart would outrun
my tongue, and flood my feelings.
Instead, it can only mutter in the dark,   1030
broken, and shattered by grief.
What hope do I have of unraveling
some solution from my burning mind?

(Enter Clytemnestra from the doors)

1022: According to some myths, this legendary healer was the son of
Apollo and the mortal Coronis. Asclepius was taught medicine by the
centaur Chiron and was killed by Zeus' thunderbolt for bringing men
back from the dead.

CLYTEMNESTRA:

1035   You must come inside, too, I mean you, Cassandra.
        Zeus in his mercy, has ordained that you share
        the holy water of this house. We have many slaves
        like you, come and join them at the household hearth.
        Step down from the chariot, this is no time for pride,
1040   even the son of Alcmene was once sold into slavery
        and had to break the bread of bondage.
        If Necessity should decree such a course,
        it is better to have masters of ancient wealth,
        for those who become suddenly rich,
1045   reaping an unexpected abundant harvest,
        are cruel and excessively punish their slaves.
        From us you will receive the customary treatment.

CHORUS:

        She's speaking to you. It's very clear
        you are caught in the net of Destiny.
        Be persuaded if you can. Will you not go?

CLYTEMNESTRA:

1050   If her language is not unlike the chattering of a swallow,
        some unintelligible barbarian speech, then I hope
        I can make her see sense and persuade her with reason.

CHORUS:

        Go in with her, it is the best choice you have.
        Do what she says, get up and leave the chariot.

CLYTEMNESTRA:

1055   I do not have time to waste by the door with her!
        Hestia's sheep are already standing

1040: This is Heracles, the son of Zeus and the mortal Alcmene. After
being driven mad and murdering his family Heracles was forced to
serve Eurystheus of Argos and undertake his famous twelve labors.

1056: The goddess of the hearth. New slaves were inducted into the
household by a ceremony at the hearth. There was also a custom in Argos
of extinguishing the hearth fire when the head of the family died and re-
lighting it to mark a new succession. Her cult was maintained by the
women of the house and was usually the first to receive any offerings.

at the center-stone awaiting sacrifice,
a joy that I never thought would come.
As for you, are you going to do as I say?
Then quickly come on!

(*Cassandra remains.*)

      Do you understand what I say?   *1060*
Well if you cannot speak, at least give me some barbarian
 sign!

CHORUS:
 I think this foreigner needs an interpreter.
 She's like a freshly caught wild animal.

CLYTEMNESTRA:
 She is mad! Her frenzied mind is full of evil.
 She has come from a city just conquered,   *1065*
 and she will not learn to bear the bridle,
 until her spirit has been broken in blood and sweat.
 I will not waste any more words to be insulted like this.

  (*Exit Clytemnestra through the doors*)

CHORUS:
 I will not be angry, I pity her.
 Come, poor girl, step down from the chariot,   *1070*
 give in to your fate and try on the yoke.

  (*Cassandra leaves the chariot.*)

CASSANDRA:
 Apollo!
 Apollo!

CHORUS:
 Why scream to Apollo?
 He does not hear songs of pain.   *1075*

1072: Cassandra sings lyrics while the chorus speaks. (See metrical
analysis in Introduction.)

CASSANDRA:
Apollo!
Apollo!

CHORUS:
Again she cries, more bad omens.
Apollo does not heed the lament.

CASSANDRA:
1080   *Apollo! Apollo!*
God of the ways my destroyer!
How easily you destroy me again.

CHORUS:
It's in her mind, she can see her own terrible future.
She may be a slave, but she still has the god's gift.

CASSANDRA:
1085   *Apollo! Apollo!*
God of the ways, my destroyer,
where have you brought me?
What House is this?

CHORUS:
The House of Atreus, do you not know?
I'm telling you the truth.

CASSANDRA:
1090   *No! No! It is the House that hates the gods!*
A witness to the murder of kinsmen! Butchery!
Manslaughter! The floor is drenched in blood.

CHORUS:
This stranger is like a dog tracking a scent.
She smells the stench of blood and blood she will find.

1079: Traditionally Apollo hears the Paean, the song of communion between mortals and gods.

CASSANDRA:

> *I have witnesses, here, I believe them.* 1095
> *I hear crying, the cries of babies butchered!*
> *Charred flesh served up to a father.*

CHORUS:

> We know all about your skill in prophecy.
> We don't want prophets here.

CASSANDRA:

> *Oh gods, what is she plotting?* 1100
> *What vast new agony? What huge horror*
> *lurks in the House? What evil plotting?*
> *The family cannot bear it, there is no cure,*
> *and help is so far away.*

CHORUS:

> I cannot understand these prophecies. 1105
> But I knew the first, the whole city screams it.

CASSANDRA:

> *You wretched woman! How can you do this?*
> *Your own husband who shared your bed.*
> *You bathe him, cleanse his body, how can I reveal the end?*
> *It shall be soon. She stretches her hands out,* 1110
> *one after another, drawing him in.*

CHORUS:

> I do not understand, first riddles and now this.
> You are confusing me with your dark prophecies!

CASSANDRA:

> *No! No! What vision is this?*
> *I see a mesh of death.* 1115
> *A net, it shares the bed, shares the blood!*

1097: Cassandra alludes to Thyestes' feast. Atreus invited his estranged brother Thyestes to a meal of reconciliation. But Atreus killed Thyestes' children and served them in a stew to their unsuspecting father (see lines 1583–1602).

Let the merciless mob descend on this family
and sound this sacrifice with a vengeful song.

CHORUS:
    What fury is this you call to howl
1120   *over the House? Your words are unclean.*
    My heart is steeped in saffron
    with the drops of my pallid blood.
    Like a man speared in battle, the sun
    sets on a fading life and quickly comes destruction.

CASSANDRA:
1125   *Look! There, look! Protect the bull from the cow.*
    The tangling conniving robes. She strikes!
    The black horn gores through!
    He falls face down in the water.
    Murder! Treachery! Dead in his own bath!

CHORUS:
1130   *I am no judge of prophecy*
    but I know this is evil.
    What good word ever
    comes to men from prophecies?
    The sayings of seers chime with evil.
1135   *The prophets teach men to know terror.*

CASSANDRA:
    Oh the pain! The agony of my fate.
    It is my pain that floods out now.
    Why have you brought me here in all my misery?
    Of course, to share his death. Why else?

1119: Now the chorus begin to sing in lyrics as well. (See metrical analysis in Introduction.)

1121: See notes for lines 239 and 612 for the importance of "steeped saffron."

1129: Cassandra continues the sacrificial imagery surrounding the death of Agamemnon introduced by Clytemnestra at 958.

CHORUS:
> You are mad! Possessed by some god,   1140
> singing this discordant song for yourself.
> You are like a nightingale, always calling
> a mind full of misery, mourning, calling,
> "Itys, Itys,"
> surrounded by sorrow, a life steeped in grief.   1145

CASSANDRA:
> The nightingale, oh for her song, her fate.
> The gods clothed her in wings and gave
> her a sweet life without further pain.
> The double-edged cleaver waits for me.

CHORUS:
> Where do these prophecies come from?   1150
> What god sends you these futile fits of pain?
> Why does your song resound with terror?
> Your droning sorrow clashing with piercing cries.
> Who laid out this path of evil
> that your unlucky prophecies follow?   1155

CASSANDRA:
> The wedding, the wedding of Paris, it destroyed my family!
> Oh Scamander, river of my homeland,
> you nursed me once, I grew up at your banks.
> And now beside Cocytus, river of the dead,
> and the banks of Acheron, hell's waterway,   1160
> I'll soon be chanting my prophecies.

1144: According to legend the nightingale was once Procne, an Athenian princess who married Tereus, a barbarian king. Tereus raped Philomena, Procne's sister, cutting out her tongue and imprisoning her so that she would not be able to reveal the crime. But Philomena wove a message on a tapestry to her sister, who took revenge by killing her son by Tereus, Itys. The gods intervened and turned Procne into the nightingale whose call was said to be for Itys, Philomena into a swallow, with its distinctive chattering call (see line 1050), and Tereus, pursuing the sisters with a sword, into the hoopoe with its long sharp beak.

1160: The two rivers of Hades.

CHORUS:
> The words you sing are so clear
> a child could understand.
> I am gripped with deadly pain,
1165
> it breaks my heart to know
> your fearful fortune, to hear your pitiful cries.

CASSANDRA:
> The agony, the agony of my city, utterly destroyed!
> All the sacrifices my father made,
> all the herds of cattle, the flocks of sheep,
1170
> slaughtered under our towers.
> There was never a hope, never a cure,
> to heal the city's suffering.

CHORUS:
> Again, the same strains as before.
> Some malicious evil spirit is crushing you,
1175
> forcing you to sing this melancholic melody,
> the song that sounds the dead.
> Is there no end to it?

CASSANDRA:
Now my prophecies will no longer hide
behind a veil, like some newly wedded bride.
1180
I can feel it rushing, swooping like a fresh wind
into the rising sun, surging like waves
into the light, revealing a fate far worse than mine.
No more riddles beguiling your minds,
bear witness, follow me closely,
1185
I shall pick up the scent of ancient wrongs.
Over this House is a deadly chorus,
chanting together, their ugly melodies.
They have sucked the blood of men and grown more daring.
They besiege this House, they cannot be driven away,
1190
seeping in, howling their horrible hymn—the Furies!
Over and over droning the song of age-old destruction.

1178: Here Cassandra stops singing and speaks to the chorus.

They spit in disgust on the bed of a brother,
they hate the defiler!
Have I missed the mark, am I not on target?
Or perhaps you think that I am a liar, 1195
a false seer, hawking her babbling prophecies?
Swear to me, admit it, I know the ancient crimes of this
    House.

CHORUS:
How could an oath do anything to help soothe you?
But, I'm amazed you know so much, even though
you have come to a foreign city from far across the sea. 1200
You speak as though you were here when it all happened.

CASSANDRA:
It was Apollo, the prophet god, he gave me this power.

CHORUS:
Can it be? A god? Did he fall in love with you?

CASSANDRA:
Once I was ashamed to speak of this, but not now.

CHORUS:
We can all have principles when things go well. 1205

CASSANDRA:
He was like a mighty wrestler, breathing passion.

CHORUS:
And did you bear his child?

CASSANDRA:
I promised I would be his, but I cheated him of that.

CHORUS:
Had the power of divination already possessed you?

CASSANDRA:
Yes, and I warned my countrymen of the suffering that was
    coming. 1210

CHORUS:
Then how did you escape the anger of Apollo?

CASSANDRA:
Once I had wronged him, I could persuade no one. They
believed nothing.

CHORUS:
But your prophecies seem so true to me.

CASSANDRA:
Ah! Ah! The agony! The pain of my true prophecies,
1215   whirling around inside my head!
Forebodings of pain seize me again!
Look! There look! Can you see them, the young,
there, in front of the house, like an image from a dream?
I can see children killed by kin,
1220   hands delving into their own flesh and blood.
I can see it clearly now, the guts and intestines,
wretched handfuls! And the father, he tasted them!
Someone is plotting revenge for all of this,
a cringing lion, lounging on the man's marriage bed,
1225   roaming his halls, watching for the master's return.
My master whose yoke I wear, I am his slave,
the commander of the fleet, the sacker of Troy,
he does not know how this detestable bitch
licks him with lengthy praise and whines her welcome,
1230   only to work her evil like a treacherous spirit of Ruin.
Such an obscenity, the woman murders the man!
What name to call this hateful fiend?
Amphisbaena—snake with venom at both ends,
Scylla—perched on the rocks, luring sailors to their deaths,
1235   a furious hell-raised mother, a merciless spirit,

1220: Cassandra sees a vision of the slaughtered children of Thyestes.

1233: A mythical serpent with a head at each end of its body.

1234: A monster with six heads that lived in caves opposite the
whirlpool Charybdis. She devoured six of Odysseus' men in Book 12 of
Homer's *Odyssey*.

breathing war on her loved ones. And how she cried out,
bold and brazen, as if she'd turned the tide of battle,
and she seemed so happy at his safe return—to her.
If I cannot persuade you it doesn't matter, it makes no
  difference,
what will be will be. Soon enough you will be standing here   *1240*
and will admit, in pity, that my prophecies were all too true.

CHORUS:
Thyestes' feast, the eating of his own children's flesh.
I understand and it makes me shudder with terror
to hear the truth so plainly spoken.
But the rest of it, I am lost, I don't understand.   *1245*

CASSANDRA:
I say you will see Agamemnon dead!

CHORUS:
Don't say such things! Poor girl, your words wound.

CASSANDRA:
Nothing can heal these words.

CHORUS:
No, not if what you say is true, god forbid!

CASSANDRA:
You pray while others commit murder?   *1250*

CHORUS:
What man devises this terrible act?

CASSANDRA:
You have strayed so very far from the path of my prophecy.

CHORUS:
I cannot see who would plot to do such a thing.

CASSANDRA:
And yet I know the Greek language all too well.

CHORUS:
   So does the oracle at Delphi, but that is just as hard to under-
1255   stand.

CASSANDRA:
   Ai! His fire rises up inside me!
   Oh Lycian Apollo! Ai!
   She is a lioness reared up on two legs.
   She beds the wolf while the noble lion is away.
1260   She will kill me. She mixes my poison, brewing my reward,
   and as she sharpens the blade meant for the man,
   she boasts of how she will exact her vengeance,
   and kill me too, for being brought here, by him.
   Why am I wearing these mockeries of myself,
1265   this staff, these garlands of prophecy around my neck?
   At least I will destroy you before I die!

      *(She tears the garlands from her neck and throws her prophet's
      staff down on the ground.)*

   Die! Die! Die! I will smash you! That is my revenge on you!
   Give someone else the riches of your misery.
   Look can you see? It is Apollo himself, he is here,
1270   stripping me of my prophet's robes.
   He saw me ridiculed, wearing these robes of his,
   laughed at by friends, turned enemies, for no reason but this.
   I was like a vagrant going from door to door,
   enduring the names: Beggar! Wretch! Scrounger!
1275   And now the prophet has finished with his prophetess,
   and has brought me here to meet my death.
   Instead of my father's altar, an execution block waits for me,
   it will soon flow red with my warm blood as I am sacrificed.
   But I will not die ignored by the gods,
1280   for there will come another to exact vengeance.
   He will kill his mother and avenge his murdered father.

1255: Apollo's seat of prophecy was the sanctuary at Delphi, the great
Panhellenic shrine in the foothills of Mt. Parnassus in central Greece
and the scene for the opening of *The Furies*.

1257: Apollo is invoked in his guise as the averter of disaster. The term
"Lycian" may stem from Apollo's function as a god of initiation.

An exile, a wanderer, estranged from his homeland,
returning to crown the destruction of his kin.
For the gods have sworn a great oath,
that his father's butchered corpse will pull him home.   1285
Why? Why then should I cry?
I have seen my city of Troy meet its end,
and her captors judged by the gods.
I will be brave, I will go in and face my death,
though these are the gates of hell.   1290
I pray, let death come in one clean stroke,
without a struggle,
let my blood flow away in an easy death.
Let me just close my eyes and sleep.

CHORUS:
Poor girl, such suffering, yet such wisdom.   1295
You have told me so much, but if you can foresee
your own death, how can you walk to the altar so bravely,
like some sacrificial cow driven by the gods?

CASSANDRA:
There is no escape, my friends, no more time.

CHORUS:
But surely it is the last few moments that are so precious?   1300

CASSANDRA:
My time has come, I have nothing to gain from running
    away.

CHORUS:
Well, you are certainly brave, you have a courageous mind.

CASSANDRA:
The fortunate never hear praise like that.

CHORUS:
But there is at least some glory in a dignified death?

CASSANDRA:
Oh my father, you and your noble children.   1305

(She approaches the door, then reels back in terror.)

No!

CHORUS:
What? What is it, what terror drives you back?

CASSANDRA:
No! No!

CHORUS:
What is it? What horror fills your mind?

CASSANDRA:
Murder! The House reeks with bloody slaughter!

CHORUS:
1310   But that is only the smell of the sacrifice at the hearth.

CASSANDRA:
It is the smell of an open grave.

CHORUS:
That must be the Syrian incense coming from the House.

CASSANDRA:
I must go inside this House now and mourn
Agamemnon's death and my own.
1315   Enough of life. Oh my friends, I am not scared,
like some bird startled from a bush,
bear witness to my death and hear my words.
A woman will die for a woman—for me,
and a man for a man who was wedded to woe.
1320   Do this for me, your guest, as I prepare to die.

CHORUS:
You poor girl, I feel so much pity for you and your
    Destiny.

1312: Pungent Eastern incense was burned at sacrifices.

CASSANDRA:
    One last word, a final lament for me.
    I pray to the Sun, the last time I will see his light,
    that when the avengers come to kill my enemies,
    may they also avenge my death, a slave, an easy victim.   *1325*
    So much for human fortune. When all is well,
    a mere shadow can turn it upside down,
    in the face of calamity, the slightest blow destroys,
    like a wet sponge blotting out a drawing.
    I do not pity myself, I pity mankind.   *1330*

    (Exit Cassandra through the doors)

CHORUS:
    One who is prosperous always hungers
    for more, all men are the same.
    No man will stop prosperity entering
    his halls, even though he has plenty,
    and say, "Enough! No more!"   *1335*
    And this man, the blessed gods
    gave him Priam's city to plunder,
    And brought him home, covered in the glory of heaven.
    But now he must pay for the blood his ancestors shed,
    and his death will cause other deaths in turn.   *1340*
    What man can say that he is ever free from
    the spirit's grip, once he has heard this story?

    (The cries of Agamemnon are heard from inside the house.)

AGAMEMNON:
    Ai! Death strikes deep!

CHORUS:
    Silence! Someone cries out, someone has been struck down!

AGAMEMNON:
    Ai! Again! Struck down dead!   *1345*

1331: The chariot may have been wheeled off here.

(The chorus splits into twelve separate voices.)

CHORUS:
 Our King cries out in agony! It has been done!
 Quickly, we must decide what to do, common action!

 —I'll tell you this, we should raise the alarm,
  get the people to storm the palace!

1350 —No! We must go in now, catch them red-handed,
  while the blade is still dripping.

 —Yes, you are right. I vote for action,
  let's do it now, there is no time to waste!

 —Wait! Can't you see what they are doing?
1355 This is the first step towards tyranny.

 —Come on! We're wasting time, the killers trample caution,
  their plans will be well advanced by now.

 —I don't know what to do, where to turn!
  We must have a plan of action.

1360 —Yes, I agree, we must first have a plan,
  words won't bring the dead back to life.

 —What! So you would surrender to tyrants,
  who defile our royal House, just to live a little longer?

 —No! Never! I could not bear to suffer that!
1365 I would rather die than be ruled by tyrants!

 —Wait! Can we assume that the man is dead
  on the evidence of these screams?

 —We should be certain of the truth before we act,
  we must not guess, we must be sure.

1370 —Then we all agree; we must first discover
  how things stand with Agamemnon.

(*Enter Clytemnestra from the doors. She stands amid the
corpses of Agamemnon and Cassandra, which are shrouded in
an embroidered robe.*)

CLYTEMNESTRA:
Words, so many words I have said to serve my needs,
and now, finally, I am not ashamed to speak openly.
How else could I have hung high the vicious nets
and caught my hated enemy in the inescapable trap,   1375
all the while pretending friendship?
So long my mind has been preparing for this,
this trial of an ancient vendetta. Now the day has come,
I stand here where I struck, and the deed is done.
This was my work, I do not deny it,   1380
he could not have escaped his destiny.
I cast my vast net, tangling around him,
wrapping him in a robe rich in evil.
I struck him twice and he screamed twice,
his limbs buckled and his body came crashing down,   1385
and as he lay there, I struck him again, a third blow
for Underworld Zeus, the savior of the dead.
He collapsed, gasping out his last breath,
his life ebbing away, spitting spurts of blood,
which splattered down on me like dark sanguine dew.   1390
And I rejoiced just as the newly sown earth rejoices,
At the nourishing rain sent by Zeus!

That is how things stand, elders of Argos,
rejoice with me if you wish, the glory is mine.

1371: The bodies may have been displayed on the *ekkyklema*, wheeled
out from the doors.

1387: The third libation was poured for Zeus Soter—"The Savior" (see
note for line 284). Clytemnestra perverts this ritual to mark the death of
Agamemnon. Hades, the god of the underworld, was also known as
Chthonic Zeus or Underworld Zeus.

1392: Zeus is primarily the Sky God who sends rain to fertilize the
earth. This image of blood-rain continues Clytemnestra's invocation at
969–72. To her, Agamemnon's death is a harvest of revenge for the
death of Iphigenia, which serves to restore her vision of natural order.

1395   If there were a libation I could pour over his corpse,
          I would be right to do it. Yes right!
          But he brimmed the cup so full of curses and evil
          that he drank it dry himself when he came home.

CHORUS:
          I am amazed at your brazen tongue, that you dare
1400   to say these things, standing over your dead husband?

CLYTEMNESTRA:
          Am I on trial like some senseless woman?
          I don't care if you praise me or blame me,
          it makes no difference to me.
          Here lies Agamemnon, my husband, dead,
1405   the work of this right hand a just craftsman.
          And that is the end of that.

[Strophe 1]

CHORUS:
          Woman! Have you eaten some kind of noxious herb?
          Has an evil potion from the sea driven you insane?
          How could you have done this? The citizens will curse you!
          You cut him down and cast him away,
1410   *now you will be cast from the city, an exile,*
          a figure of hate, reviled by the people, despised.

CLYTEMNESTRA:
          Now you pass judgment! Exile from this land,
          the hatred of the people, public curses.
          But him! What charges did you ever bring against him?
1415   For all he cared he might as well have been killing an animal.
          Oh, he had plenty of sheep to choose from,
          but he sacrificed his own child, my labor of love,
          to charm away the cruel storm-winds of Thrace.
          He was the one you should have banished from this land,

---

1406: The chorus responds in sung lyrics while Clytemnestra delivers
her justification in strong measured marching anapests (see metrical
analysis in Introduction).

as punishment for the pollution he brought on us.   *1420*
But when you hear of what I have done,
you judge so harshly. Go on, threaten away!
I'll meet your match. If you overthrow me, then you win,
but if the gods have ordained another outcome,
then you will learn discretion, however old you are.   *1425*

[Antistrophe 1]

CHORUS:
Megalomania! Such brazen speech.
You must be mad! Crazed by the killing,
I can even see blood streaked in your eyes!
No one will stand by you, you have no allies.
Revenge will come and you will pay, blow for blow.   *1430*

CLYTEMNESTRA:
Listen then to my oaths, sanctioned by what is right.
By the justice I exacted for my child,
by Ruin, and the Fury in whose honor I sacrificed this man.
My hopes will never tread the halls of fear,
as long as my hearth-fire is kept alight   *1435*
by Aegisthus, loyal as ever, to me.
He is like a shield to my confidence.
Here he lies, the adulterer, he wronged me,
seducer of every little Chryseis at Troy,
and there she lies, his prize won by the spear,   *1440*
his prophetess and prostitute,
his faithful fortune-telling bedmate,
and how many sailors' benches she must have lain on!
Both have received their just reward.
He lies there, and she like a dying swan, she sang   *1445*
her last lament, and now she lies here too,
another delicacy, a luxury for my feast. What lovers!

1436: The only surviving son of Thyestes, Clytemnestra's lover and co-conspirator.

1439: The daughter of the prophet Chryses. Chryseis was captured during the Trojan War and awarded to Agamemnon as a war prize. She was returned after Apollo cursed the Greeks with a plague.

[Strophe 2]

CHORUS:
> *Oh let me die now, quickly, free of pain,*
> *no bedridden, lingering illness for me.*
1450   *Let Destiny bring my death,*
> *and bring me the sleep that has no end,*
> *now that our kind guardian has fallen.*
> *He endured so much for the sake of a woman,*
> *now a woman's hand has struck him dead.*

1455   *Oh demented Helen,*
> *you wasted all those lives,*
> *under the walls of Troy,*
> *now you are crowned with the final victory.*
> *But the blood will never wash away,*
1460   *the spirit of destruction lives here, in this House,*
> *a deep-rooted agony that crushes man.*

CLYTEMNESTRA:
> Do not pray for Destiny to bring death
> bearing the burden of all this.
> And don't turn your anger on Helen
1465   as the destroyer of men, she was just one woman,
> as if she alone killed so many Greek men!
> She did not cause these incurable wounds.

[Antistrophe 2]

CHORUS:
> *You spirit that has cursed this House,*
> *and the twin descendants of Tantalus,*
1470   *your power surges through the souls of women,*
> *an evil power that tears my heart.*

1469: The father of Pelops, and originator of the line that bred Agamemnon. Tantalus was punished by the gods for testing them by feeding his son to them in a feast. Pelops was saved by Demeter and bought back to life, but Tantalus paid the price by being eternally "tantalized" and never being allowed to eat or drink, with nourishment kept just out of his reach.

> *Look at you, perched over the dead,*
> *like some hateful raven, croaking*
> *your discordant gloating hymn.*

CLYTEMNESTRA:
So now your thoughts are stated correctly,   *1475*
you call on the triple-gorged spirit
that plagues this family,
the one that lusts to fill its belly with blood.
And even before old wounds have healed
the infection comes again and out seeps new pus.   *1480*

[Strophe 3]

CHORUS:
> *Yes, the spirit has a mighty grip*
> *on this house, such unrelenting anger.*
> *Oh, such a vicious trail of destruction,*
> *an insatiable appetite for disaster.*
> *Oh! Oh! The will of Zeus,*   *1485*
> *cause of all, doer of all.*
> *What do mortals ever accomplish without Zeus?*
> *What part of this have the gods not ordained?*

> *Oh, my king, my king, how should I mourn you?*
> *How can I tell you how much you were loved?*   *1490*
> *Lying there in this spider's web,*
> *you have drawn your last breath,*
> *such a sacrilegious death.*
> *Oh, to see you shamed like this,*
> *struck down with a double-edged blade,*   *1495*
> *by the treacherous hand of your own wife.*

CLYTEMNESTRA:
So you confidently claim that this was my work
but do not call me Agamemnon's, no!
For I am the age-old spirit of vengeance
in the guise of this dead man's wife.   *1500*
I have repaid the debt of Atreus,
the giver of that obscene banquet,
and I have sacrificed this full-grown victim,

in payment for the slaughtered young.

[Antistrophe 3]

CHORUS:
1505   *And you say that you are innocent of his murder?*
Do you have a witness? How can you?
No, but I can believe that you were helped
by the ancestral spirit of vengeance.
The dark spirit of slaughter wades through a torrent
1510   *of this family's blood, Ares is forcing ahead*
to take his revenge for the children, butchered
for that feast, their dark blood, long congealed.

Oh, my king, my king, how should I mourn you?
How can I tell you how much you were loved?
1515   *Lying there in this spider's web,*
you have drawn your last breath,
such a sacrilegious death.
Oh, to see you shamed like this,
struck down with a double-edged blade,
1520   *by the treacherous hand of your own wife.*

CLYTEMNESTRA:
He did not die a sacrilegious death!
Wasn't he the one who used treachery
and brought ruin down on this House?
Yes, he has suffered, deed for deed,
1525   for what he did to our daughter,
Iphigenia, his own flesh and blood!
I have cried so many tears for her.
He had better not make any proud boasts down in Hades,
for he has paid with his own death for what he began.

[Strophe 4]

CHORUS:
1530   *Which way to turn? I can't think,*
I am so confused, this makes no sense.
What can I do? The House is falling, I am so frightened.
Thunder shakes the House, and the drops of blood

that fell before turn torrential and rain down hard.
The sword of Justice is being sharpened   1535
on the grindstone of Destiny to cut more pain.

Oh Earth, Earth, if only you had taken me under
before I saw my king lying here,
laid low in this silver-walled bath.   1540
Who will bury him? Who will sing his lament?
Will you dare to do it, to sing his mourning song?
You who killed your own husband, will you
try to atone his spirit with your empty tributes?   1545
Hollow homage for a life of greatness!
Who will sing praises over his tomb?
Who will shed tears for this godlike man,
with any true feeling in their heart?   1550

CLYTEMNESTRA:
   That is none of your business!
   We killed him and we will bury him,
   deep down under the earth;
   this House will not mourn for him.
   Iphigenia, his daughter,   1555
   as is right, will meet her father
   at the crossing of the swift sea of death,
   and she will throw her arms around him,
   and she will kiss him.

[Antistrophe 4]

CHORUS:
   Blame is met with blame,   1560
   it is so hard to decide between them.
   The plunderer plundered, the killer killed.
   But while Zeus sits on the throne,
   the wrongdoer suffers, that is the sacred law.
   Can the progeny of this curse be cast from the House,   1565
   or is this family welded to its own destruction?

CLYTEMNESTRA:
   And now finally you can see that the prophecy
   was true. I am willing to make a pact

with the spirit of the Pleisthenids.
1570   I shall accept that what's done is done,
even though it is hard to bear,
and in return it must leave our House,
to take its evil to some other family
and destroy them with kin-killing misery.
1575   I will live modestly and will be content,
if I can rid these halls of this frenzy of death.

> *(Enter Aegisthus and armed men from the stage right wing.
> Aegisthus mounts the stage and stands beside Clytemnestra,
> as the guards deploy in the orchestra in front of the stage.)*

AEGISTHUS:
Welcome bright day of justice!
Now I know that the gods look down
on the crimes of mortal men, and exact vengeance.
1580   Here he lies, a delight to my eyes,
shrouded in a robe woven by the Furies,
paying the price for his father's revolting crime.
Atreus, once ruler of this land, was this man's father,
and the brother of Thyestes, my father.
1585   In a struggle for power, Atreus had driven
him away from his home and city.
Poor Thyestes returned, a suppliant at his own hearth,
thinking he would be safe, and so he was;
his blood did not stain our ancestral ground.
1590   Atreus, the godless father of this man,
playing the generous host, staged a false festival.
He seated each man apart and served up
to my father a feast of his own children's flesh.
Their heads and hands and feet were hacked
1595   into pieces and thrown into a boiling stew,
from which he, in ignorance, ate his fill.
A meal that brought the curses upon this House!
When he discovered the obscene truth, he screamed
out in horror, reeled back from the table, kicking it over

1569: Some myths name Pleisthenes as the actual father of Agamemnon and Menelaus, saying that he died young, leaving them in the care of their grandfather, Atreus.

and, retching, vomited up the butchered flesh. 1600
Then he shouted out his curse upon the sons of Pelops,
"Damn to death the clan of Pleisthenes!"
That is why this man lies dead.
I planned his killing, with Justice at my side.
I was the youngest child and just a babe in arms 1605
when my father was driven from his home.
I grew up in safety, abroad until Justice brought me back.
I was in exile, but the enemy could not escape my grasp,
mine was the making of this fatal plot.
Now I could go happily to my grave, seeing him 1610
lying here, tangled in the nets of Justice.

CHORUS:
Aegisthus, you are contemptible, you revel
in this misery. You say that you killed this man
in cold blood, that you alone planned his pitiful death.
Then you will not escape Justice nor the people's curses, 1615
they will cast their stones and you will surely die.

AEGISTHUS:
You dare to speak to me like that,
you, who man the oars down below?
We are the helmsmen and masters of this ship.
A lesson in discretion can be hard for the elderly, 1620
the scourge, chains, and a starving old stomach
are most excellent teachers of understanding.
Do you have eyes in your head? Can you not see?
The more you fight your fate, the more you will suffer.

CHORUS:
Woman! You skulked at home, while the other men 1625
went to war, all the time you were fouling this man's bed,
plotting the death of our commander.

AEGISTHUS:
Such sentiments breed grievous tears.
Well, you're certainly no Orpheus, are you?

1629: The son of Apollo and one of the Muses, Orpheus was famous for
his musical genius, which charmed all, including the Sirens and Hades.

1630   He led all to pleasure with the sound of his voice,
        you only infuriate me with your idle yelping.
        So I'll lead you away, to be broken and mastered.

CHORUS:
        As if you could ever be the master of Argos!
        You who plotted the death of our king,
1635   and did not even dare to do the deed yourself.

AEGISTHUS:
        Because the deception was clearly woman's work,
        I was a suspect, an enemy known of old.
        But with his wealth I shall try to rule his people,
        and if anyone disobeys me I will yoke him
1640   to a heavy harness, and he will not be treated
        like a well-fed trace-horse, no, hateful hunger
        and a dark cell will see him buckle under.

CHORUS:
        Why did you not kill the man yourself?
        You coward! Why did a woman murder him
1645   and stain the land and its gods?
        Oh, Orestes, if he still sees the light of day,
        may good fortune bring him home,
        may he kill this pair and be the final victor.

AEGISTHUS:
        Well, if that is your wish, you'll soon be taught a lesson.

CHORUS:
1650   Stand ready, friends, arm yourselves!

             (*Aegisthus addresses his guards.*)

1635: The killing of Agamemnon by Clytemnestra may have been a
dramatic innovation on the part of Aeschylus. In Book 4 of the *Odyssey*,
it is Aegisthus who is named as having actually murdered the man, although Clytemnestra is cast as Aegisthus' lover and assists with the
deception.

AEGISTHUS:
Draw your swords, men!

CHORUS:
I am ready. I am not afraid to die.

AEGISTHUS:
So you want death, do you? Then you shall have it!

(Aegisthus' guards move toward the chorus.)

CLYTEMNESTRA:
No, my dearest, no more killing.
We already have a wretched harvest to reap.   1655
No more bloodshed, enough!
Venerable elders, please go home before you come to
   harm.
What we did had to be done.
If only this could be an end to our troubles,
the spirit has held us in its talons long enough.   1660
That is the word of a woman if any care to heed it.

AEGISTHUS:
But these men, their mouths spit insults at me.
You are pushing your luck hurling abuse at me.
It would not be discreet to spurn your new master.

CHORUS:
Argive men would never bow before a villain like you.   1665

AEGISTHUS:
Don't you worry, I will have my way in the days to come.

CHORUS:
Not if the spirit brings Orestes home.

AEGISTHUS:
Exiles feed on hope, we all know that.

CHORUS:
Go on! Grow fat, defiling Justice, while you still can!

AEGISTHUS:

1670   I promise you, you will pay for your insolence and stupidity.

CHORUS:

Yes, boast while you feel brave like a cock beside his hen!

CLYTEMNESTRA:

Don't listen to them and their idle yelping. You and I hold
the power of this house. We will set things right once and for

1672   all.

> *(Exit Clytemnestra and Aegisthus through the doors. Exit
> chorus through the stage right wing)*

-END-

1672: The tableaux of Agamemnon and Cassandra may have been
moved back behind the doors at the exit of Clytemnestra and Aegisthus, with the doors closing ominously behind.

The Libation Bearers

The mother's curse, the hellhounds of hate, they are here!
(1054)

Cast of Characters

ORESTES	son of Agamemnon and Clytemnestra
PYLADES	his friend, son of Strophius of Phocis
ELECTRA	his sister
CHORUS	of Eastern slave women
DOORMAN	for the household of Aegisthus
CLYTEMNESTRA	queen of Argos
CILISSA	Orestes' old nurse
AEGISTHUS	ruler of Argos
SERVANT	to Aegisthus and Clytemnestra

The Libation Bearers

SCENE 1: *The tomb of Agamemnon in Argos, seven years later.*

> *(Enter Orestes and Pylades from the stage left wing into the orchestra)*

ORESTES:
> Hermes of the underworld, guardian of my father's power,
> be my savior, stand with me in the pursuit of my claim.
> I have returned to my land, I have come home.
> Father, I call on you, here at your tomb,
> hear me, father! Heed my words!   5
> To River Inachus, my nurturer, I offer a lock of hair,
> and I lay another here as a mark of my grief.
> I was not here, father, to mourn your cruel death,
> I could not pay you homage as you lay on the bier.

> *(Enter the chorus of black-robed slave women from the stage right wing into the orchestra)*

Opening: The orchestra altar may well have served as Agamemnon's tomb.

1: Hermes, the son of Zeus and Maia, is invoked in his guise as escort of the dead and spiritual guide.

6: The main river of Argos.

10   Look! There, do you see? A band of black-clad
women making their way towards us?
What does this mean?
More misery for the House?

     (The chorus draws nearer to the tomb.)

No, I think they are bringing libations for my father,
15   to soothe his sprit beneath this earth.
Yes, I am sure of it, look there! I can see Electra,
my sister. She is with them, marked by her grief.
Zeus! Give me revenge for the death of my father!
Be my ally, and fight at my side!
20   Pylades, let's hide. We'll keep clear and discover
why these women make this supplication.

     (Orestes and Pylades move toward the stage.)

[Strophe 1]

CHORUS:
Sent from the House to bear libations,
heavy hands, beating hard.
Cheeks marked with crimson, gashed,
25   *nails plough furrows, fresh and deep.*
For all this life my heart has fed
on tortured cries of grief,
sorrow sounds the tearing
of threadbare fabrics,
30   *sullen folds clothe the breast*
that nurture our despair.

[Antistrophe 1]

A hair-raising scream, a fierce
sleep-breathing cry from the prophet,
a shriek in the dead of night.

21: Large funeral processions with hired professional mourners had been a feature of Athenian death rites among the aristocracy. However, at some point in the late sixth or early fifth century, legislation was passed limiting the scale and excessiveness of these ceremonies.

Terror swept the halls of the House 35
and fell hard upon the women's rooms.
And the dream diviners,
pledged by the gods to know,
blamed the wrath from those below,
and told of the malice 40
the killers had stirred.

[Strophe 2]

Oh Gaia! Earth-Mother!
This is an empty gesture to ward off evil. 45
That godless woman sends me here,
I fear to let her words be heard.
What can redeem blood once spilled?
Oh miserable hearth!
Oh destructive House! 50
There is no sun, only hateful gloom,
desolate darkness envelops the House,
where a master was brutally killed.

[Antistrophe 2]

The unconquerable majesty, untamed, invincible, 55
that once filled the hearts and minds of the people,
is gone now, cast aside
instead there is only fear.
Happiness is a god, even more than a god, 60
but the scales of Justice tilt suddenly,
for those who bask in the light,
for those who dwell in the shadows,
for the powerless shrouded by the night. 65

[Strophe 3]

Nurturing Earth has drunk too much blood,
the gore of vengeance congeals, it will not drain away.
agonizing ruin infects the guilty,
sickened by devastating suffering.

44: One of the earliest divinities, nurturer of life, recipient of the dead
and the daughter of Chaos.

[Antistrophe 3]

70   *Nothing can remedy the virgin's defilement,*
     not even all the rivers of the earth, flowing
     together in one great torrent, could cleanse
     the stain of murder from tainted, bloody hands.

[Epode]

75   *The gods forced their fate on my city.*
     Destiny took me, from the home of my father,
     to lead this life of slavery.
     The just and the unjust I must abide,
     and force my will to master
80   *the bitter hatred in my mind.*
     I shed tears behind a veil,
     for the unnatural end of my master.
     My blood creeps cold with secret grief.

ELECTRA:
     Servant women, keepers of the House,
85   my escort in these rites of atonement,
     now I need your advice.
     When I pour these burial offerings, what should I say?
     What would be right? How can I pray to my father?
     Should I say I bring dedications from a loving wife
90   to her beloved husband, when they come from my mother?
     Or should I recite the customary saying:
     "Repay those who send these honors,"
     for they deserve a gift that matches their evil.
     Should I pour them away in silence and disgrace,
95   just as my father died, and let the earth drink them dry?
     Or should I throw this vase behind me, just discard it,
     then avert my eyes and just walk away?
     I do not have the courage! What should I say
     as I pour these liquids on my father's tomb?
100 Give me your counsel, dear sisters, we share
     a bond of common hatred in this house, open your hearts,

---

77: The chorus are slaves, possibly captive Trojan women, certainly
hailing from the East.

don't conceal your thoughts, you need have no fear.
Destiny's day draws near
for both the free and the slave,
tell me if you know a better way.   *105*

CHORUS:
Your father's tomb is like an altar to me,
as you have asked, I will speak my mind.

ELECTRA:
Then speak out of respect for my father's grave.

CHORUS:
As you pour, praise those who are loyal.

ELECTRA:
Which of my friends can be called that?   *110*

CHORUS:
First, yourself, and then all those who hate Aegisthus.

ELECTRA:
Then I should say this prayer for me, and for you?

CHORUS:
That is for to you to decide, you must learn the answer.

ELECTRA:
Who else can I place on our side?

CHORUS:
Remember Orestes, even though he is far away.   *115*

ELECTRA:
A good thought, you were right to remind me.

CHORUS:
Then be mindful of those guilty of murder.

ELECTRA:
What should I say? Teach me, show me the right way.

CHORUS:
Pray that some spirit or a man may one day come.

ELECTRA:
120   Do you mean to judge or to exact justice?

CHORUS:
Simply state one to kill those who killed.

ELECTRA:
But is it right to ask this of the gods?

CHORUS:
How could it not be right to repay your enemy, evil for evil?

ELECTRA:
[165]   Mighty herald of above and below,
Hermes of the underworld, summon me
125   the spirits from beneath the earth,
let the sentinels of my father's House hear me.
Call the Earth-Mother who gives all things life,
grows them strong, then receives again their harvest.
As I pour this holy water for the dead,
130   I call to my father: take pity on me, bring back
dear Orestes, rekindle the light of this House.
Now we live no better than refugees,
sold by our mother in exchange for a man,
Aegisthus, her partner in your murder.
135   I live like a slave, and Orestes is banished
from his inheritance, while they revel
in the luxurious fruits of your labors.
May the turn of fortune bring Orestes home!
This is my prayer, hear me, father,
140   grant me the discretion my mother lacks,
keep my hands clean and pure.
These prayers are for us, for our enemies I say:
bring the avenger into the light,

123: The manuscript places this line at 165, but most scholars place it here.

let Justice kill the killers!
In the midst of my prayers for good,   145
I say for them a prayer for evil.
Send us your blessings, send them up high,
let gods, Earth and Justice bring victory!
These are my prayers as I pour this libation.
Sound the death cry to flower my prayers,   150
sing the invocation in honor of the dead!

    (Electra pours the libation.)

CHORUS:
Let the tears splash, falling,
for a fallen master,
splashing this bastion to evil.
We pour these libations   155
to avert the pollution.
Hear me, hear me, royal master,
your spirit gripped by darkness.

Ototototototo!
Let him come, a man of the spear,   160
a liberator of the House,
his Scythian bow bent back,
Ares' death-bolts ready,
he closes in, sword in hand.

ELECTRA:
The earth has drunk the libations poured for my father.

    (Electra sees the lock of hair on the tomb.)

But wait! There is something new, here.   166

151: Electra, guided by the servant women, turns an offering contrived by Clytemnestra to appease the dead into a call for vengeance.

162: Scythia was the name used for the region spreading from the Danube to the Caucasus. The area provided archers for Athenian forces in the sixth century. The bow may have been regarded primarily as a weapon associated with hunting and the young male initiate.

CHORUS:
Tell me, my heart throbs with foreboding.

ELECTRA:
Someone has laid a lock of hair on the tomb.

CHORUS:
Does it come from a man or a young girl?

ELECTRA:
170   That is easy, anyone could guess.

CHORUS:
How? The youth must teach her elders.

ELECTRA:
I am the only one who could have cut this lock.

CHORUS:
Yes, those that should mourn, can only hate.

ELECTRA:
And yet it looks very much like ...

CHORUS:
175   Like what? Tell me.

ELECTRA:
Like my hair, it looks exactly like mine.

CHORUS:
Could it be a secret offering from Orestes?

ELECTRA:
It does look like his hair.

CHORUS:
But how could he dare to come here?

ELECTRA:
180   He has sent this lock of hair to honor his father.

CHORUS:
  Then we have all the more reason for tears:
  this means he will never again set foot in this land.

ELECTRA:
  A sickening wave surges over me,
  an arrow strikes and pierces my heart,
  my eyes shed torrents of thirsty tears,   *185*
  falling relentlessly like a winter storm.
  And as I gaze at this lock, how could I imagine
  that any other could claim title to this?
  The killer could not have cut it,
  my mother, who turned her profane mind   *190*
  against her own children, against her very name.
  But how can I accept that this offering
  could have come from my dear Orestes?
  Oh! Hope is fawning on me.
  If only hope had the clear voice of a herald,   *195*
  then my whirling mind would not be torn in two.
  I would know for sure that this lock was severed
  from the head of an enemy and I should cast it out,
  or that it came from a kinsman, laid in sympathy,
  adorning this tomb in honor of my father.   *200*
  We call on the gods; they know the storms
  that send us spinning like sailors on the high seas,
  and if by some happy fate we are delivered,
  even the smallest sapling can grow into a mighty tree.

       (Electra sees footprints on the ground.)

                                                                  205
  Another sign! Look at these tracks,
  a pair of footprints, they are like mine.
  There are two sets of marks here, his own,
  and these must be his companion's.
  Look at the marks left by the heel and the sole,
  they are the same as mine, the same size ...   *210*
  This is agony! All reason is destroyed!

       *(Orestes moves toward the altar and presents himself to
       Electra.)*

ORESTES:
Your prayer has been fulfilled, proclaim it to the gods
and pray for the future, praise your good fortune.

ELECTRA:
Why? What has divine grace ever given me?

ORESTES:
215   You see the sight you have prayed for.

ELECTRA:
How can you know my prayers?

ORESTES:
I know about Orestes and how he fills your heart.

ELECTRA:
But how have my prayers been answered?

ORESTES:
Here I am, I am your nearest, your dearest.

ELECTRA:
This is a trick, and you are a stranger trying to trap me in
220   your net.

ORESTES:
Then I am plotting against myself.

ELECTRA:
Are you mocking me in my misery?

ORESTES:
If I mock your misery, then I mock mine.

ELECTRA:
Then, should I call you—are you really—Orestes?

ORESTES:
225   You still do not realize though you see me yourself,
yet, when you saw the lock I had cut in mourning,

and were following the tracks of my steps,
your heart raced at the thought of seeing me.
Take the lock and hold it next to the place it came from.
You see? It is your brother's, the same as yours. 230

(He shows her a small piece of woven fabric.)

Look at this weaving, the work of your hand,
the strokes of your shuttle, the animal motif.

(Electra begins to react joyously.)

Control yourself! Don't loose your mind for joy.
Our closest kin are both our cruelest foes.

ELECTRA:
You are the closest and dearest to your father's House. 235
How I wept for you, the seed of hope, salvation!
Be bold, be strong, win back the House of your father!
Bright-eyed joy! Four loves in one for me.
It is right to give you the name of our father,
and the love I should have felt for mother, 240
I turn to you, for I most justly hate her.
Yours is the love for my sister, savagely sacrificed,
and as my faithful brother you paid me honor.
Let Power, Justice, and Zeus the Third,
mightiest of them all, stand at your side. 245

ORESTES:
Zeus! Zeus! Behold our cause!
Look on the brood bereft of their eagle sire,
who died entwined in the coils of a vicious viper.
Look on the starving orphans, ravaged by hunger,
too young to carry their father's prey to shelter. 250
Here you see Electra and Orestes,
children robbed of their father,
both outcasts, exiled from our own House.

232: The nature of this weaving is uncertain from the text. Perhaps it is
something like a family crest. Fabric, such as the tapestry and net, plays
a significant role throughout the trilogy.

Our father sacrificed and paid you great honor.
255   If you destroy his nestlings who will serve
your lavish banquets, as he once did?
If you destroy the eagle's brood,
man will never again believe your signs.
If the royal tree withers and dies,
260   your altars will be ignored
on the day the bulls are sacrificed.
You can rebuild the House to former glory,
raise and restore it from a pile of ruins.

CHORUS:
Speak softly, son and daughter, saviors
265   of your father's hearth, you may be overheard,
rumors can be spread and reach the ears
of those in power. I wish them dead,
and to see their blood boiling in the flames.

ORESTES:
The great oracle of Apollo will never betray me,
270   it is his mandate that I should endure this trial.
His shrill prophecies wrenched my guts and chilled
me to the bone, they foretold storms of suffering
if I did not avenge my father's killers.
He said to kill the way they killed,
275   and claim my birthright like a savage bull,
or pay the penalty myself with a life
gripped by evil, and full of pain.
He revealed to me the malicious rancor
that festers below and infects mankind,
280   the malignant sores that thrive on flesh,
their scurvy jaws devouring the natural health,
pallid fur sprouting from the putrid pus.
He told of the onslaught by the avenging Furies
the progeny of a father's spilled blood.
285   How, from the darkest depths, the death-bolt

261: A king was appointed by Zeus (see *Agamemnon*, line 45) as high
priest of his people. He presided over sacrifices that were the chief form
of communion between mortals and gods.

would pierce, as the murdered kin beg for revenge.
Insanity and paranoia would haunt the night,
visions of scowling faces peering from the gloom,
tormented and deranged, driven from cities,
a body battered by the brazen scourge. 290
The cup of fellowship can never be shared,
and the thank-offering cannot be poured.
Dragged from altars by a father's unseen wrath,
none can offer shelter, there can be no sanctuary,
just a lonely death, disgraced and despised, 295
wasting away, reduced to nothing.
These then were the oracles, how could I not act on them?
Even if I did not, the deed must still be done,
I have many motives of my own that drive me:
the god's command, the great sorrow I feel for my father, 300
and the burden of my stolen birthright.
And what of my people, the finest of men,
who conquered Troy with their sterling spirit?
They should not be ruled by a pair of women!
Yes, he's a woman at heart, we'll soon see that for ourselves. 305

CHORUS:
Mighty Destinies come,
fulfill the will of Zeus,
Justice veer the course,
words of hate fulfill hateful
words. Justice screams
and demands her price. 310
Bloody blow pays bloody
blow. "The doer suffers,"
sounds the saying, three times old.

[Strophe 1]

ORESTES:
Oh father, sad father! 315
What to say, what to do,
to soar your distant spirit
from the death bed's tight
embrace? Can light transcend
the darkness? This lament 320

will grace you with some honor,
son of Atreus, lying here.

[Strophe 2]

CHORUS:
   Child, the ravenous jaws of fire
325 *can never quell the spirit dead,*
   in time the rage will surely flare.
   Our death-rattle batters
   to make the harm appear,
   to rouse your father, your creator.
330 *All wail the vendetta song,*
   that stirs, and seeks the sin.

[Antistrophe 1]

ELECTRA:
   Now father, hear my grief,
   I add my voice, my tears.
   Two children at your tomb
335 *to chant the dirge of death.*
   Receive at your grave
   the exile and the suppliant.
   What is good? What is evil?
   Can we ever conquer Ruin?

[Epode]

CHORUS:
340 *But if the gods desire, we may yet*
   sing a sweeter sounding strain.
   Not death-wails beside the tomb,
   for the song of invocation will fill the halls of kings,
   filling the loving cup to toast the restitution.

[Strophe 3]

ORESTES:
345 *If only at Troy,*

Father, a Lycian spear
had cut you down.
Your legacy would glorify the House,
and the name of your children
would be met with respect.   350
Your tomb would stand high
in a land across the sea,
no burden for this House to bear.

[Antistrophe 2]

CHORUS:
He'd be welcomed by comrades,
his men who fell with honor.   355
He'd be first beneath the earth,
a majestic, stately prince,
a minister for the mighty,
who rule the realm below.
He was a king while he lived,   360
his authority the Destinies ordained,
the sovereign scepter was his to hold.

[Antistrophe 3]

ELECTRA:
No, never at Troy
father, death beneath the walls,
lying beside the war-dead,   365
buried by Scamander's straits.
I wish instead, your killers
had died your despicable death,
then in every place the people
would learn of their fate,   370
and this pain we'd never know.

346: A region in southwestern Asia Minor. The Lycians were allies of
the Trojans and led by Sarpedon.

[Epode]

CHORUS:
> Child, your dreams gleam brighter than gold,
> a treasured fortune, beyond the northern winds.
> You have the power to speak of great things,
375 > but the crack of the double lash stings deep.
> We have our allies beneath the earth,
> though power is held by those we hate,
> their hands are tainted, they are unclean.
> It is you, the children, who will seize the day!

[Strophe 4]

ORESTES:
380 > That strikes the ear,
> piercing like an arrow.
> Zeus, Zeus, force vengeance
> up from below, rain down Ruin
> on depraved and defiant hands.
385 > Fulfill the debt we owe the parents.

[Strophe 5]

CHORUS:
> Let me be first to yell
> the hallowed call, flaring up
> as the man is struck
> and the woman dies.
> Should I hide what's deep inside,
390 > hovering in my mind? Bitter
> blasts rage before my heart,
> my savage soul seethes with spite.

[Antistrophe 4]

ELECTRA:
> And when will Zeus
395 > clench his fist and strike them?

373: This is the land of the Hyperboreans, a legendary people who were said to lead perfect lives.

Yes, yes, shatter their skulls!
Restore this land's faith.
I want Justice from injustice.
Hear me earth, and powers below.

CHORUS:
It is the law, that spilled blood soaking   400
the ground demands blood in return.
Murder screams for the Furies
to stand for those long dead,
to bring on Ruin in the trail of Ruin.

[Strophe 6]

ORESTES:
Oh you infernal powers!   405
Look you curses of the dead!
Look at the last of Atreus,
helpless, homeless, and shamed.
Which way to turn? Help me, Zeus!

[Antistrophe 5]

CHORUS:
My heart shudders   410
to hear this despair,
I lose all hope,
it repels my blood
darkening within.
But the pain relents,   415
as new hope dawns
in all her radiant beauty.

[Antistrophe 6]

ELECTRA:
What should our prayers be saying,
that we suffer the pain of our parents?
She tries to fawn, we'll not be charmed,   420
like savage wolves, we'll not be tamed,
no mother comfort soothes our rage.

[Strophe 7]

CHORUS:
> *We beat the Persian death-wail,*
> *the way of the Cissian wailing-woman,*
425 > *clenched fists splattering blood,*
> *hands stretching higher, reaching,*
> *smashing, crashing, the blows rushing,*
> *pounding against my wretched head.*

[Strophe 8]

ELECTRA:
> *Oh cruel, shameless mother,*
430 > *bitter bier that bore him.*
> *The king denied to his people,*
> *the man denied his wake.*
> *How could she bury him unmourned!*

[Strophe 9]

ORESTES:
> *He was humiliated and disgraced,*
435 > *but she will pay for my father,*
> *by the will of the spirit,*
> *by the will of these hands.*
> *I will do away with her, then I can die.*

[Antistrophe 9]

CHORUS:
> *He was mutilated of manhood,*
440 > *and she buried him like this,*

424: An area of Persia surrounding the city of Susa in what is now southwestern Iran. Excessive displays of mourning were associated with the East.

439: The practice of *maschalismos* involved cutting off the genitalia of a murder victim and hanging them under the armpits before burial. This was a method of rendering the corpse powerless to avenge itself.

to ensure that his death
would be too hard to bear.
Know the dishonor done to your father.

[Antistrophe 7]

ELECTRA:
You speak of my father's death,
but I was shut away, worthless,
confined to chambers like a dog.   445
Laughter died and how I wept,
secret tears of forbidden grief.
Hear me! Carve it on your mind.   450

[Antistrophe 8]

CHORUS:
Let this prick your conscience
keep a fixed mind, be strong.
It stands just as it stands,
You burn to know the rest.
Steel you hearts and go with Rage.   455

[Strophe 10]

ORESTES:
I call you father, stand with your kin.

ELECTRA:
Through the tears I ask this of you.

CHORUS:
We come together we echo the call.
Hear us! Come into the light!
Stand with us against the hated!   460

[Antistrophe 10]

ORESTES:
Force meet force, right meet right!

ELECTRA:
> *Gods, fulfill our rights with justice!*

CHORUS:
> *I shudder to hear these prayers.*
> *Doom's day has long been waiting.*
465 > *Let it come, let the prayers be answered!*

[Strophe 11]

> *The agony of generations.*
> *The blood-soaked blow.*
> *The pandemonium of Ruin.*
> *The cruel, insufferable grief,*
470 > *such unrelenting pain.*

[Antistrophe 11]

> *The House can be healed,*
> *but not from outside,*
> *the cure is found within,*
> *savage, brutal bloodshed.*
475 > *Gods below, this is your hymn!*

[Epode]

> *Hear us, blessed powers of the earth,*
> *answer our prayers, send us your help,*
> *guide your children to their victory!*

ORESTES:
> Father, you were denied a kingly death.
480 > Hear me! Give me power over the House.

ELECTRA:
> Father, help me, help me destroy
> Aegisthus, help to set me free!

ORESTES:
> Then your rightful feast-day can be founded,
> or else the savory flesh charred for the earth
485 > will starve you of honor while feeding the dead.

ELECTRA:
  And I will pour my dowry out to you,
  I'll bring wedding wine from my father's store,
  first and foremost to revere your tomb.

ORESTES:
  Oh Earth, raise my father to watch my fight!

ELECTRA:
  Oh Persephone, give us your beautiful power!   490

ORESTES:
  Remember the bath, that bathed you in blood.

ELECTRA:
  Remember the net they devised to trap you.

ORESTES:
  Fettered in chains not made of metal.

ELECTRA:
  That shameless, deceitful shroud.

ORESTES:
  Father, awake and answer this disgrace!   495

ELECTRA:
  Father, dear father, hold up your head!

487: Under Athenian marital custom, a fatherless girl was given in marriage by her nearest male relative. Electra recognizes Orestes as her guardian, not Aegisthus. Therefore, she cannot be married until he reclaims his ancestral house. The bride received a dowry from her guardian to help support her new family.

490: Persephone was the daughter of Zeus and Demeter and the wife of Hades. She spent half of the year in the underworld and half with her mother above. She is thus associated with the renewal of the seasons and the restoration of life.

ORESTES:
  Send Justice to fight at our side,
  give us the match, hold for hold.
  For your defeat we'll throw them down.

ELECTRA:
500 Hear me, father, one last cry,
  look at your fledglings, nestling at your tomb,
  pity the male and female, pity your children.

ORESTES:
  The House of Pelops must survive;
  dead but not dead, your memory lives with us.
505 The children sustain the dead man's name,
  like buoyant corks lining a net,
  saving the mesh from sinking to the depths.

ELECTRA:
  Hear us! This lament is for you.
  Heed our words, save your honor.

CHORUS:
510 No one could find fault with your words,
  this tomb, his fate, they have never been mourned.
  Now your minds are set, it is time for action.
  You must put the spirit to the test.

ORESTES:
  Yes, and I will not stray from this path, but tell me
515 why she sent these libations? What compelled her,
  after so long, to try to soothe this incurable wound?
  It is a paltry offering to send the unconscious dead.
  What kind of gifts are these? They fall so short
  of her crime, what was she thinking?
520 "Pour everything out for the blood you have shed
  you're wasting your time in appeasing the dead."
  Do you know why she did it? Can you explain it?

CHORUS:
  I know, my son, I was there: she had terrible dreams,

terror stalked her nights, she shook with fear,
and so that godless woman sent these libations.   *525*

ORESTES:
Do you know what the dreams meant, can you tell me?

CHORUS:
She dreamed she gave birth to a snake, she said it herself!

ORESTES:
A snake? What else?

CHORUS:
She laid it down, and wrapped it like a baby.

ORESTES:
What? Did she see this creature feeding?   *530*

CHORUS:
She dreamed that she suckled it herself.

ORESTES:
But, a snake? It must have slashed her breast?

CHORUS:
It sucked her milk, clotted with blood.

ORESTES:
It has its meaning, the snake represents a man.

CHORUS:
She screamed in her sleep and woke shaking with fear.   *535*
Torches flared up, burning away the blind darkness,
and lamps lit the halls to comfort the mistress.
She sent these libations to appease the dead,
hoping for a cure to cut away her affliction.

ORESTES:
I pray to the earth and to the tomb of my father,   *540*
that this dream finds fulfillment in me.

I can see it now, it all falls into place.
The snake came from the same place as I.
She wrapped it in the same cloths that I wore.
545   It suckled at the breast that nurtured me,
fouling her precious milk with clotted blood,
and this sight made her scream in terror.
As she has raised this gruesome omen,
so she must die. I am the snake,
550   I will be the one to kill her and fulfill this dream.

CHORUS:
Then you are my prophet, I believe your interpretation.
Let it be as you say. Let your friends play their part.
Tell us what you need us to do.

(Pylades moves toward Orestes and Electra.)

ORESTES:
The plan is simple. My sister must promise
555   to keep our meeting secret and go back inside.
They used stealth to kill a man of honor,
and so by stealth they will die, trapped
by the same snare. So Apollo has ordained,
and the prophet god has never yet proved wrong.
560   I will take what I need and dress like a stranger.
This is Pylades, an ally, a friend to our house,
he and I will go together to the gates.
We both know the Parnassian dialect,
so we will sound like men from Phocis.
565   The doorkeepers may well turn us away,
after all, an evil spirit dwells in that House,
then, we simply wait, so that anyone passing by
the House will assume the worst and say:
"Why does Aegisthus shut his gates to guests?
570   Is he at home? Does he know these men are here?"
Once in, across the threshold, I'll find him
sitting there on my father's throne.
He'll come to meet me, face to face,
I'll fix his stare and he'll look away,

563: Mt. Parnassus overlooks Delphi and the area known as Phocis.

then before he can say "Where are you from?" 575
he'll be a corpse, on the end of my swift sword.
The Fury, with its unquenchable thirst for death,
will drain a third cup of thick, pure blood.

Electra, you must keep a close watch in the House
for this plan to be successful and turn out well. 580
You women, make sure you hold your tongues,
keep silent and speak only when you need to.
For my part, I call on my father here
to steady my sword as I leave for the fight.

(*Exit Orestes, Pylades, and Electra through the stage right
wing*)

[Strophe 1]

CHORUS:
The Earth nurses countless creatures, 585
hideous fiends, gruesome beasts.
The Sea cradles terrible monsters,
infested waters that poison man.
The Sky is streaked by deadly lights
that break the shackles of heaven. 590
The bird on the wing and the beast
of the field know well the raging
storm-winds of god-sent wrath.

[Antistrophe 1]

But who can explain men
and their audacious minds? 595
Or the reckless thoughts of women,
the brazen lust that consummates
the marriage of mortal ruin?
A seduction of loveless lust,
that perverts and overwhelms 600
both man and beast alike.

[Strophe 2]

Those who hold right minds,

have heard of Althaea,
605   *scheming daughter of Thestius,*
and her plots, burned in the flames.
She threw in the fire the bloody torch,
saved from the time the infant first cried.
The life of the torch for the life of the child,
610   *until Destiny marked the day*
when life burned away.

[Antistrophe 2]

There is another hateful legend,
the story of Scylla, bloody bitch,
615   *enticed by her enemies with gold*
to murder her own dear father.
Lured by the gift of Minos,
a golden necklace from Crete,
620   *she cut the magic lock of Nisus.*
He slept and drew his last breath
as Hermes came and took him in death.

[Strophe 3]

As I recount these bitter stories
I remember a loveless marriage,
625   *one that cursed a House.*
Plots connived in the mind of a woman,
against the man, the warrior,
against the man, feared by foes.

605: The mother of the hero Meleager, who was told by the spirits of Destiny that her son would live only as long as a brand on her fire. Althaea removed the brand and kept it safe until she learned that Meleager had killed his brothers. In a fit of rage she threw the brand on the fire, destroying her son.

614: The daughter of Nisus, the mythical king of Megara, which lay to the west of Attica. Nisus had a purple lock of hair that served to protect his city. Scylla was seduced by King Minos of Crete, an enemy of the Megarians. Bribed with a necklace, she cut off the lock of Nisus, which destroyed her father and betrayed her city to its foes.

A House dishonored, a stone-cold hearth,
ruled by a womanly, cowardly spear.   630

[Antistrophe 3]

The Lemnian story is first among evils,
a hideous tale of abject atrocity.
The name of Lemnos is burned in disgrace,
the title for each new vile crime.
Fouled by the guilt, detested by the gods,   635
banished from mankind, their strain died out.
No one respects what is despised by gods.
Which of these stories was I wrong to tell?

SCENE 2: *The House of Atreus in Argos.*

> *(Enter Orestes and Pylades from the stage right wing into the
> orchestra)*

[Strophe 4]

The sword rips through the lungs;
the keen blade, wielded by Justice,   640
tears down deep. Right has been wronged,
for they overstepped the mark,
respect for Zeus was trampled underfoot.   645

> *(Orestes and Pylades mount the stage and approach the doors.)*

[Antistrophe 4]

The anvil of Justice is rooted firm,
Destiny has already forged the sword.
The child is brought home to pay the debt

630: This is a reference to Aegisthus (for the importance of the hearth
in the rightful transfer of power, see the note for *Agamemnon* line 1056).

631: The Lemnian women murdered their husbands in a fit of jealousy.

638: The exit of Orestes, Electra, and Pylades at 584, the preceding information, and the intervening choral song followed by the entry of
Orestes and Pylades onto the stage would have been sufficient to mark
the scene change from the tomb of Agamemnon to the House of Atreus.

650   *by the ever scheming, infamous Fury.*
       The stain of bloodshed will be cleansed.

              (*Orestes knocks on the doors.*)

ORESTES:
       Boy! Boy! Can't you hear me knocking at the door?
       Is anybody there! Boy! Boy! Is anyone at home?
655   For the third time, will someone come out,
       if Aegisthus welcomes strangers to this house?

       (*The doorman's voice is heard from within the house*)

DOORMAN:
       All right! All right! I can hear you. Who are you and where
          are you from?

ORESTES:
       Tell the heads of this house that I am here,
       I have come to see them with fresh news.
660   Be quick about it! Night's dark chariot
       races on, and it is time for the traveler
       to put in at a house of hospitality.
       Have someone in authority come out,
       the mistress in charge, though the man
665   would be more fitting. Feminine delicacy veils
       words in obscurity, man to man, a conversation
       is confident, with plain speaking and straight talk.

              (*Enter Clytemnestra from the doors*)

CLYTEMNESTRA:
       Strangers, please, your needs are our pleasure,
       we have all you would expect from a house
670   such as this, warm baths and soft beds to soothe
       your cares away, and honest eyes to watch your sleep.
       If there are other matters, needing more serious consideration,
       then that is a task that must be shared between men.

ORESTES:
       I am a foreigner, a Daulian from Phocis.

674: Daulis was a city near Delphi in Phocis.

Now at journey's end I can unyoke my feet and rest. 675
I was on my way, pack and all, to Argos
and I came across a stranger, another traveler.
We told each other where we were going, and as we talked
I learned his name, Strophius the Phocian.
He saw I was Argos bound and asked me to do him justice 680
by delivering this message: "Orestes is dead."
He stressed that I must be sure to tell his parents
and to inquire whether his family would want him home,
or if he should lie buried in the land where he lived,
an eternal guest, a migrant in a foreign land. 685
He asked that I convey their wishes back to him.
His remains are now encased in a bronze urn,
and Strophius said that his loss was deeply mourned.
I've told you all I heard, but I should really be speaking
to the head of the house. I must inform his parents. 690

CLYTEMNESTRA:
Oh! We are besieged by ruin!
Oh damned curse that grips this House!
Nothing escapes your gaze, your deadly bolts
fly so very far, nothing is out of harm's way.
You strip me of my loved ones, plunge me into despair! 695
And now Orestes, though he had the sense
not to set foot in this swamp of destruction.
Now Hope has gone, the one cure
for these evil, maddening rites.
Condemn Hope as a traitor, Hope has betrayed us!

ORESTES:
I wish that I could have come to know the comforts 700
of such an affluent house by bringing good news.
Where can we find more kindness than the ties
that bind the guest and host? But to my mind
it would have been a breach of a sacred duty
not to have performed this obligation for a friend. 705
I gave my word and was bound by the code of hospitality.

679: See *Agamemnon,* line 880 and note.

CLYTEMNESTRA:
Be assured you will receive no less than you deserve,
nor be any less a friend under the roof of this house.
We would have soon heard the news all the same.
710   Following the long day's journey, the weary traveler
should rest. It is time you were made at home.
Women, show this man to the guest rooms,
take his traveling companion with him,
let them enjoy the hospitality of this house.
715   It is your responsibility; they are in your charge.
I will share this news with the head of the house,
and we will consult our many friends,
as we consider this turn of events.

(Exit Orestes, Pylades, and Clytemnestra through the doors)

CHORUS:
Sisters, women of the House,
720   *when will we have the power*
to speak out for Orestes?
Sacred earth, sacred mound
that entombs the Sea Lord,
covering the corpse of a king.
725   *Now hear us! Now help us!*
Now is the hour of stealthy Persuasion
to come and stand at his side.
Come Hermes, come Night,
guide the work of his deadly sword.

(Enter Cilissa, the nurse, from the doors)

Look there, Orestes' old nurse is coming out, crying.
730   It seems the stranger is about his vile work.
Where are you going, Cilissa?
Why are you crying?

CILISSA:
The mistress has ordered me to summon Aegisthus
735   as quickly as I can. He must come and hear the news,
man to man, so it'll be clear. In front of us servants
she was all doom and gloom, but her eyes were smiling
deep down, at what had worked out well for her.
But not for the House, no, it's the curse, I know it,

the news those strangers brought made that clear, 740
and I'll bet he'll be overjoyed when he finds out.
Oh the misery of it all! All the old pain mixed together,
right here in this House of Atreus, it's too much to bear.
It breaks my heart to think on it.
But this, I've never known agony like this, 745
I withstood all the other troubles, flushed them out,
but my dear Orestes, I spent my soul on him,
and I raised him when his mother passed him to me.
I never complained, even though his screaming
would keep me up half the night, I worked 750
my fingers to the bone for him, all for nothing!
A baby's like a little animal, it can't think for itself,
it needs to be nursed. You have to know its mind.
I mean, when he was that small he couldn't talk,
so he couldn't tell me if he was hungry, or thirsty, 755
or when he wanted to pee, and a baby's insides are a law
unto themselves, let me tell you! I had to foresee
his every need, and a lot of the time I was wrong,
then I would have to wash his little baby clothes.
Washerwoman and child-minder all rolled into one, 760
I was an expert at both, a real professional,
which is why Orestes' father entrusted him to me.
Now they tell me he is dead and I've suffered it all.
So I have the task of fetching the man who fouled
this House, and see him rejoice to hear this news. 765

CHORUS:
How did she tell him to come?

CILISSA:
What do you mean? Say that again, I don't understand.

CHORUS:
Will he be bringing his guards or coming alone?

CILISSA:
She said that he should bring his guards.

CHORUS:
No, don't tell the master that, not if you hate him. 770

Tell him instead to come alone, quickly,
and be cheerful so that he will not be suspicious,
the messenger can make the warped word straight.

CILISSA:
What! Are you happy to have heard this news?

CHORUS:
775   Why not? Zeus can avert an ill wind.

CILISSA:
How can that be? Orestes is gone, this House has lost all
    hope.

CHORUS:
Not yet. It would be a poor prophet who predicted that.

CILISSA:
What do you mean, do you know something that I don't?

CHORUS:
Go now, take your message, follow your orders.
780   The cares of the gods are for the gods to take care of.

CILISSA:
Then I'll go and do what you want
and with the help of the gods may it be for the best!

(*Exit Cilissa through the stage right wing*)

[Strophe 1]

CHORUS:
Now I pray to you, Zeus,
father of the Olympian gods.
785   *Grant good fortune to the rightful*
rulers of the house, who yearn
to see discretion rule.
I call out in the name of Justice,
Zeus protect her, guard her well.

[Mesode 1]

Zeus, Zeus, guide him into the halls,   790
and set his enemies before him.
If you raise him to greatness
you will be generously repaid,
a double measure, no, a triple reward!

[Antistrophe 1]

You see the young colt of the man you loved;   795
he is yoked to a chariot of suffering.
Set a measured pace on his course,
sustain his steady stride,
let us see him come around
the final homeward bend.   800

[Strophe 2]

You inside the House, reveling
in your luxury, do you hear!
Hear me, sympathetic gods,
pay the debt of past bloodshed
with this just, fresh slaughter.   805
Then may the House be purged
of the murders known of old.

[Mesode 2]

Apollo of the beautiful chasm,
let this man raise his household's head,
let its loving eyes peer out
to gaze upon the light of freedom
from behind the dismal veil.   810

[Antistrophe 2]

Help us, Hermes,
child of Maia.

807: At Delphi, Apollo's seat of prophecy, there was believed to be a deep chasm over which the priestess sat and was influenced by the power of the Earth rising up from below.

813: Daughter of the Titan Atlas and one of the Pleiades. Maia means "mother" or "nurturer."

He can veer a favoring course,
815 *reveal the unseen,*
speak the hidden words.
He can bring to day the dark of night
and dim their eyes with shrouded sight.

[Strophe 3]

And when the House is set free,
820 *we women will raise our voices,*
high and loud, strong and steady,
and sing the blessing of fine, fair winds:
"The ship sets sail and all is well!"
825 *We all will prosper, we'll share the gain,*
Ruin will leave us and go far from our friends!

[Mesode 3]

When the time comes for you to act,
be strong. When she cries out, "My child!"
Say, "My father's child!" and do the deed.
830 *You won't be blamed for the course of Ruin.*

[Antistrophe 3]

Place the heart of Perseus in your breast,
repay the debt of those you love,
those that lie beneath the earth,
and those who still stand on it.
835 *Go inside against the Gorgon,*
loose Ruin on her murderous spree,
behold the guilty, and then destroy.

(Enter Aegisthus from the stage right wing)

831: A legendary hero who was sent to kill Medusa the Gorgon, a female monster who could turn men to stone. Perseus decapitated Medusa with the help of Athena and Hermes.

835: The myth of Perseus and the Gorgon was closely connected with the initiation rites of young men.

838: It may have been that this entrance occurred earlier in the choral song, in order to give the actor playing Aegisthus time to enter the orchestra from the deep wing and even to mount the stage.

AEGISTHUS:

I was told that I should come and hear the news.
Apparently a stranger has arrived with the message,
that Orestes is dead, words I wished we would never
have to hear. How can this House bear another blow   *840*
and its murderous, festering wound not drench us in terror?
How can I tell if this really is the living truth
or just a fearful rumor spread by women,
a spark of fire flaring up that flickers and falls away?   *845*
What can you tell me about this?
I want to set my mind at rest.

CHORUS:

We have heard the story, but go inside and hear
the strangers for yourself. The power of a message
can never equal firsthand news from the man himself.   *850*

AEGISTHUS:

I want to see this messenger and question him again.
I want to know if he witnessed the death in person,
or if he is repeating some vague rumor he's heard.
I'll not be fooled, my mind sees with sharp eyes.

    (Exit Aegisthus through the doors)

CHORUS:

Zeus, Zeus, what should I say?   *855*
Where should I begin my prayer?
My intentions are worthy, I ask the gods for help,
but how can I find any fitting words?
Now the bloodstained blades
that cut men down are being raised,   *860*
to strike the blow that forever ends
the House of Agamemnon.
Or the son will strike the sparks of freedom's fire,
and claim the throne of this city
to inherit his father's fortune.   *865*
The challenger in this final round,
godlike Orestes, one to throw two.
Let Orestes win the victory!

    (The chorus hears a cry from behind the doors.)

AEGISTHUS:
　　Ai! Ai!

CHORUS:
870　　There! There it is!
　　What is happening, what does this mean for the House?
　　Keep back, until this terror is over,
　　We must appear blameless.
　　The fight is over, and what will be, will be.

　　　　(Enter a servant of Aegisthus from the doors)

SERVANT:
875　　No! It is the end! My master has been cut down!
　　No more, no more, Aegisthus is no more!
　　Come quickly, help me break down the door
　　to the women's rooms, we must unbar the bolts,
　　it takes the strength of a young arm, help me!
880　　It is too late for Aegisthus, he is dead,
　　but Clytemnestra! Get up! Get up!
　　I'm wasting my breath, are you asleep in there?
　　Get up! Don't you hear me, are you deaf to my shouts?
　　Where is Clytemnestra? What is she doing?
　　It is her neck on the block now, and Justice is poised to strike.

　　　　(Enter Clytemnestra from the doors)

CLYTEMNESTRA:
　　What ever is the matter? What is all this shouting in the
885　　house?

SERVANT:
　　The living are killed by the dead!

CLYTEMNESTRA:
　　I know what this riddle means,

885: It would have proved dramatically effective as well as practical
for the doors to remain open here until 930.

we killed by deceit and by deceit we die.
Quickly, bring me the man-killing axe.

(Exit servant through the doors)

Victory or defeat? We have come this far.   890
Now we will know, once and for all.

(Enter Orestes from the doors)

ORESTES:
You, I want you. He has done his part.

CLYTEMNESTRA:
No! My dear brave Aegisthus, gone!

ORESTES:
You love this man? Then share his grave
and never betray him, even in death.   895

CLYTEMNESTRA:
Wait, my child! My son, have you no feelings?
This breast once nurtured you, cradled your sleep,
your soft mouth sucked the milk that made you strong.

ORESTES:
Pylades, what should I do? How can I kill my own
    mother?

(Enter Pylades from the doors)

PYLADES:
And what then becomes of the Oracles of Apollo   900
declared at Delphi, or the unbreakable oaths we took?
Better to be hated by every man on earth than hated by the
    gods.

889: There was a tradition in art and myth that Clytemnestra killed
Agamemnon with a large, double-headed sacrificial axe.

893: The body of Aegisthus was probably not present on stage at this
point.

ORESTES:
  Your wise words have won me over, Pylades.

  (To Clytemnestra)

  Then come! I will slaughter you at his side.
905 Alive, you thought him better than my father.
  Die then! And lie with him forever, your lover!
  Since you hated the man you should have loved.

CLYTEMNESTRA:
  I was the one who raised you; let me grow old with you.

ORESTES:
  You killed my father, and now you want me to live with you?

CLYTEMNESTRA:
910 Destiny played a part in this, my son.

ORESTES:
  Then Destiny shall make your deathbed.

CLYTEMNESTRA:
  You should fear the curse of your kin, my son.

ORESTES:
  You just gave birth, then abandoned me to a life of misery.

CLYTEMNESTRA:
  I never abandoned you. I sent you to the house of an ally.

ORESTES:
915 Sold like a slave, the son of a free man.

CLYTEMNESTRA:
  Then where is the fee I received from the sale?

ORESTES:
  I am ashamed to speak of it.

CLYTEMNESTRA:
Then you should also speak of your father's vices.

ORESTES:
Do not accuse him! He endured while you sat at home.

CLYTEMNESTRA:
My son, it is hard for a woman to be kept from her husband. 920

ORESTES:
It is a man's labor that provides the home you sit in.

CLYTEMNESTRA:
My son, I think you mean to kill your mother.

ORESTES:
You are the killer, not I. You kill yourself.

CLYTEMNESTRA:
Then beware the vengeful hellhounds of a mother's curse.

ORESTES:
And how would I escape a father's if I failed? 925

CLYTEMNESTRA:
I'm crying in vain over my own tomb.

ORESTES:
The fate of my father marked out your end.

CLYTEMNESTRA:
Ah! I suckled this serpent, I gave it life!

ORESTES:
Yes, the terror you saw in your dream was true.
You should not have killed, now suffer what you should not. 930

(*Exit Clytemnestra, Orestes, and Pylades through the doors*)

CHORUS:
Mourn for this pair and their double downfall,

but let all-enduring Orestes prevail
as he ascends this mountain of bloodshed.
Let the heart of this houshold never, ever die.

[Strophe 1]

935   *Came justice at long last to Priam and his sons,*
devastating retribution, payment in blood.
Came the double lion, a double god of war,
to the House of Agamemnon.
An exile, guided by Apollo,
940   *steered by godly counsel,*
to force this to its end.

[Mesode 1]

Raise the hallowed call for our master's house!
It has escaped the evil, it has been cleansed
of the two defilers, who wore the wealth away.
945   *The House is free from its own foul fate.*

[Antistrophe 1]

Came Hermes, secret fighter
who destroys with stealth,
his fighting hand held
by the true daughter of Zeus.
950   *We call her Justice, rightly named,*
breathing destruction, hatred and rage.

[Strophe 2]

Apollo ordained it, loud and clear
from the gorge at Mt. Parnassus.
955   *He attacks by stealth, the time will come,*
by stealth the wrong will be undone.
Always somehow, the gods prevail

934: For "heart" the Greek has "eye," which was regarded as the most precious and essential part of the body.

937: The double lion is a metaphor for Orestes and Pylades.

to preserve us from these evils.
Heaven has the right to our respect.   960

[Mesode 2]

Now I can see the light,
the mighty curb that yoked the House
has been lifted. Rise up great House,
you have lain in ruins time enough.

[Antistrophe 2]

Time brings everything to fulfillment   965
as it threads the gates of this House,
cleansing the stain on the hearth,
the purifying rites driving out Ruin.
We see the face of fortune turn to favor,
the future looks bright to behold,   970
and the intruders are banished from the House.

> *(Enter Orestes from the doors, standing over the bodies of*
> *Aegisthus and Clytemnestra covered by the death shroud of*
> *Agamemnon)*

ORESTES:
Look at the double tyrants of our country,
the killers of my father, the rapists of his House.
How regal they must have been, seated on their thrones,   975
and so much in love, even now, judging by their end.
They made their vows and stood by their pledges,
together they swore to murder my father,
together they swore they would die. They kept this faith.

> *(Orestes indicates the cloth that killed Agamemnon.)*

Look at this, as you try to comprehend the evil,   980
look at this hideous contrivance that fettered my father,
the manacles for his hands, the shackles for his feet.

972: The *ekkyklema* may have been used here. This would make for an
effective dramatic parallel with the tableaux of Agamemnon and Cassandra displayed after *Agamemnon*, line 1371.

Lay it out! Gather round!
Spread out the cloth that covered the man.
985   Let the father see, not mine, but the one that sees all,
let Helios the sun gaze at my mother's foul work.
He will be my witness on the judgment day
and testify that I was right to kill my mother.
As for Aegisthus, there is no need to speak of him,
990   he died the adulterer's death as set down by law.
She plotted this abomination against the man,
she, who bore his children, carried them in her womb.
Once there was love, but now you see the hatred, the evil.
What was she? A deadly serpent, a venomous viper
995   that poisoned by touch, leaving her prey unbitten.
Such an evil, audacious mind.
And this, what words can I find to describe it?
A trap for a wild animal, a shroud of death from head to foot,
a robe from the bath to cover a coffin.
No, it is a trawling mesh,
1000   a hunting net, a garment to fetter the feet.
This is a robber's tool of the trade,
one who cheats guests and steals for gain,
luring victims with insolent stealth,
killing to gratify a treacherous heart.
1005   I would have the gods destroy me, childless,
before I shared my house with a woman like this.

CHORUS:
Ai! What horrifying work!
What an abominable way to die!
Oh! Oh!
This pain will grow bitter fruit, the survivor will suffer!

ORESTES:
1010   She did this, did she not? Mark my witness,
this shroud dyed by Aegisthus' sword.
The ravages of time and oozing blood
conspired to ruin this steeped embroidery.
Now I can praise him, now I can mourn him properly,
1015   I can speak before the weaving that killed my father.
I grieve for our family, the things that were done, the suffering.
But do not envy me, I have won a tainted victory.

CHORUS:
No mortal man lives a life free from suffering.
No one exists only with honor.
Oh! Oh!
Day after day our lives are plagued by pain.   1020

ORESTES:
I do not know how it will end.
I am a charioteer with a runaway team,
hurtling off the course, loosing grip of the reins,
loosing grip of my mind, spinning out of control.
My heart dances in terror and howls a furious tune.   1025
While I still have my sanity, know this:
I killed my mother with Justice at my side.
She was a defiled murderer, the gods hated her.
What compelled me to do this? What magic charms?
The greatest influence was Apollo's prophet,   1030
the oracle told me: "Do it and go unpunished,"
and if I had failed, the penalty defies description;
no arrow could reach the heights of those pains.
And now look at me, I have the suppliant's armor,
the olive branch and this wreath. I'll go to the sanctuary   1035
at the center of the earth, the shrine of Loxian Apollo,
where the brilliant light of the sacred flame never dims.
I must run from the blood that I shed, run from my own
     blood,
no hearth will shelter me, only Delphi, it is Apollo's will.
I charge the men of Argos with remembrance: 1040
tell Menelaus the evil things that happened here.
And now I go, an exile, banished from this land.
In life as in death, my name will always be known for this.

CHORUS:
But you have done well. Don't damn yourself
with evil words, don't let your tongue denounce you.   1045
You have liberated the entire city of Argos
by beheading two snakes with one good clean stroke.

     (Orestes imagines that he sees the Furies approaching.)

1047: The Furies are probably not present on stage at this moment.

ORESTES:
Ah! Ah!
Women, there! Like Gorgons!
Black clad, writhing with snakes!
1050   I can't stay here! I have to go!

CHORUS:
What is it? What sights whirl you into such a frenzy?
You are the son of Agamemnon, be still, don't surrender to
        fear.

ORESTES:
Not sights! These terrors are real!
The mother's curse, the hellhounds of hate, they are here!

CHORUS:
1055   It must be the fresh blood on your hands,
you are distraught, confused.

ORESTES:
Lord Apollo! They are coming! Closing in!
I can see their eyes dripping with blood!

CHORUS:
You must be purified. The touch of Apollo
1060   will free you from this torture.

ORESTES:
You can't see them, but I can, they force me away!
I must go now! Now!

        (*Exit Orestes, running through the stage left wing*)

CHORUS:
Go with our blessings, Orestes. May the god protect you
and treat you kindly. May you be granted some good fortune.

1065   *Three times the storm has struck*
and hurled its icy blasts
against this royal House.
First the feast of children's flesh,

Thyestes' tortured pain.
Then the murder of the man, 1070
the deadly bath, the death of a king
who ruled the whole Greek army.
And now the third, it comes again,
the savior or the doom?
When will it end? When will it be calm? 1075
When will it sleep, this fury, this Ruin?

(Exit the chorus through the stage right wing)

-END-

1076: The tableaux of Clytemnestra and Aegisthus may have been left on stage as the final bloody image of the play and then withdrawn behind the closing doors of the house to mark the end of the play, reflecting the close of *Agamemnon*.

The Furies

And from this time on, the race of Aegeus will forever uphold this judicial assembly. (683–4)

Cast of Characters

THE PYTHIA   priestess of Apollo

APOLLO   son of Zeus

ORESTES   son of Agamemnon and
                                  Clytemnestra

THE GHOST OF CLYTEMNESTRA   slain queen of Argos

CHORUS   of Furies

ATHENA   patron goddess of Athens

ATHENIAN CITIZENS

GROUP OF ATHENIAN WOMEN

The Furies

SCENE 1: *The sanctuary of Apollo at Delphi.*

 (Enter the Pythia from the stage right wing)

PYTHIA:
 First of the gods, foremost in my prayer,
 I honor Gaia, the Earth Mother, the first seer,
 then Themis, for it is said that she was the second
 to take her mother's place of prophecy.
 The third was Phoebe, a Titan, a daughter of the earth,   5
 her place bestowed in peace by Themis.
 Phoebe bequeathed it to Apollo at his birth,

Opening: The Pythia was the most important oracle in the Greek world. Named for the snake who was said to originally inhabit the sanctuary, she was a priestess of Apollo who served for life as a conveyer of prophetic utterances in a trancelike state. [The various myths dealing with the history of the site relate how Apollo took over the cult from earlier, female deities, perhaps representing the Olympian mastery over darker, primordial chthonic forces.]

3: Daughter of Gaia and Ouranus and the personification of divine law or "Right." She is the mother by Zeus of Justice (*Dike*), Peace (*Eirene*), and the sprits of Destiny (*Morai*).

5: Phoebe was a daughter of Gaia and Ouranus, sometimes associated with the Moon. Her name means "radiance" or "pure brilliance."

hence Phoebus, the name that honored the gift.
He left the lake and ridge-backed land of Delos
10   and landed on Athena's ship-laden shores.
On he came to this land of Mt. Parnassus
with an Athenian escort paying him homage.
They were the road builders, the sons of Hephaestus;
they cleared the way, they tamed the frontier.
15   On came Apollo, and the people revered him,
and King Delphus, hand on helm, received him with honors.
Zeus inspired, Apollo's mind swelled with the divine arts,
and he became the fourth to sit on this mantic throne,
the prophet of his father, the spokesman of Zeus.

20   These gods come first in my prayers, but Athena
who stands before the temple is foremost in my speech,
and I revere the nymphs of the Corycian rock,
the cave beloved by birds, where the spirits dwell.
I remember that Dionysus inhabits in this land,
25   ever since he marshaled the Bacchae, weaving
the Destiny of Pentheus, the death of a hunted hare.
By the river of Pleistos and the power of Poseidon,
I call on Zeus the Fulfiller, the highest god,

9: An island located in the center of the Cyclades in the Aegean Sea, the birthplace of Apollo and site of a sanctuary to the god.

10: The coast of Attica.

13: The founding father of the Athenians, Erichthonius, was the son of the god Hephaestus.

16: The legendary founder of the Delphinian people.

20: The daughter of Zeus, goddess of wisdom, crafts, and strategy, and patron of Athens.

21: The shrine of Athena *Pronaia* ("before the temple") was located southeast of the Castalian spring, where visitors would purify themselves before entering the sanctuary at Delphi.

22: A cave near the peak of Parnassus high above the sanctuary, sacred to Pan and local nymphs.

24: The son of Zeus and Semele (the Moon), god of wine, revelry, and theatre. He was said to occupy Delphi during the winter while Apollo was with the Hyperboreans.

as I go inside to take my seat as prophet.
Let this entrance surpass all times past   30
to be the best by far. If any Greeks are here
have them enter by lot, according to our custom.
Know that my prophecies are given by the god.

> *(The Pythia exits through the doors then immediately reenters,*
> *terrified and scurrying on all fours.)*

Horrors! Horrors to tell! Horrors before my eyes,
they have repelled me from Apollo's house!   35
I am terrified, my legs have frozen in fear! I cannot stand,
I have to crawl out on my hands and knees.
A scared old woman is nothing, no more than a helpless
    child.

I was entering the chamber where the wool wreaths
hang, and I saw a man by the center-stone,   40
stained in the sight of the gods and crouching
in supplication. His hands and drawn sword
are dripping with blood, and he is clutching
a tall olive branch, rightly wreathed
with a full woolen shank of silvery fleece.   45
In front of this man was an astonishing throng
of women propped against the benches asleep.
No, not women, they were a hideous sight,
more like Gorgons, but worse, much worse.
I have seen paintings of the beasts that plagued   50

26: Pentheus was the grandson of Cadmus and ruler of Thebes. According to mythology he resisted the worship of Dionysus, who had turned the Theban women into Bacchants and led them to the wilds, where they reveled in honor of the god. Pentheus was persuaded by Dionysus to spy on the women, but was discovered and torn apart by the female members of his own family.

27: The main river of Delphi. Poseidon, the god of the sea, had a shrine in the Temple of Apollo at Delphi.

40: This is the *Omphalos*, the navel stone situated at Delphi that was said to mark the center of the earth.

45: The olive branch and wool wreaths were carried by the suppliant, a mortal who had sought the protection of the gods.

Phineus and stole his food, but the creatures in there
have no wings, they are dark, dank and disgusting.
Their foul stench and hideous breath forced me back,
and their eyes seep a repulsive, putrid pus.
55   They are wrapped in black dismal rags not fit for human sight.
A place of holy idols should not suffer such an evil apparition.
I have never known a race that spawned such creatures,
nor have I seen a land that could boast to have bred them
without suffering some terrible blight—terrible pain!
60   Apollo must decide what to do with them,
he is the master of this house,
he is the healer, the prophet,
he has the power to purify a house.

> *(Exit Pythia through the stage right wing)*

> *(Enter Orestes and Apollo from the door. The sleeping Furies*
> *are barely visible in the doorway.)*

APOLLO:
I will not forsake you, I will protect you until the end,
65   I will stand by your side even when I am far, far away,
your enemies will never receive comfort from me.
You see those foul, frenzied creatures, they are trapped,
I have lulled the disgusting virgins to sleep.
They are the wizened ancient children, repugnant
70   to gods and untouched by man or beast.
The progeny of evil wallowing in misery
spewed from their infernal abyss, the bowels of hell.
Abhorred by men on earth and despised by the Olympian
     gods.
So run, run, flee these creatures, never weaken,
75   for they will drive you across continents,
to the ends of the earth, their feet pounding, on and on,
across the ocean, beyond the far seawashed lands.

51: A Thracian king cursed with blindness and stricken by the Harpies, flying female monsters that stole and fouled his food.

64: There is much debate over the entrances and exits in this scene. Some editions place Orestes and Apollo on the *ekkyklema* and do not reveal the Furies until 140.

But never stop, never weaken, you must endure
and reach the city of Athena, be her suppliant,
fall at her feet, hold her, clasp her wooden idol.   *80*
There you will find the judges of your cause,
and we will charm them with words, we will find a way
to finally free you from this ordeal. I will help you,
for it was I who persuaded you to kill your mother.

ORESTES:
Lord Apollo, you know how not to be unjust,   *85*
so learn how not to be neglectful.
You have the power for good, you can save me.

APOLLO:
Remember this, never let your mind be overcome by fear.
Hermes, paternal brother, be true to your title,
protect him, be his escort and his guide.   *90*
Be sure to guard my suppliant well,
Zeus respects the sacredness of the outcast.
Go quickly now and bring him back to the world of men.

*(Exit Orestes through the stage left wing; exit Apollo through
doors)*

(Enter the ghost of Clytemnestra)

CLYTEMNESTRA:
You sleep? What use are you asleep?
It is because of you that I am dishonored by the dead,   *95*
they charge me with the killings, accuse me,

80: A sacred olive wood sculpture of the goddess was housed in the
sixth-century Temple of Athena and Erechtheus on the Acropolis.

93: It is not known how this entrance was staged. It should not be as-
sumed that entrances following exits were instantaneous; a dramatic
pause perhaps heightened with music would have done much to enhance the eerie mood of this scene. A ghost entering from Apollo's temple would not be amiss, as it was said to stand on a sacred chasm that
led to the realm of chthonic (underworld) spirits.

and the dead are relentless in resentment.
I have no place, I am shunned in shame,
they indict me with the harshest blame,
100   I who suffered the cruelest pain from my closest kin.
There is no angry god to avenge me,
slaughtered by those mother-killing hands.
See my wounds—let them tear your hearts!

105   All those honeyed liquids and sweet libations
I poured for you, you lapped them up,
the dark nocturnal feasts I burned at the hearth,
in the dead of night, at the ungodly hour.
110   Now I see it all trampled underfoot.
He has gone, just skipped away like some fawn,
sprung from the midst of your hunting net,
turning back only to grin and mock you.
Hear me, I am pleading for my soul!
115   Mind me, underworld goddesses,
a dream of Clytemnestra is calling you.

      (The Furies stir and groan.)

You whine while your man has fled and gone.
Even suppliants have allies, I have none.

120   *(They stir again.)*

Too much sleep, not enough pity for my pain.
Orestes, the mother-killer, has escaped!

      (The Furies moan.)

You groan, yet sleep. Awake! Awake!
125   Why else do you exist if not to inflict evil?

      (They moan again.)

So fatigue and sleep have conspired
to suck the strength of the furious serpent.

CHORUS:
Hunt!
    Hunt!
       Hunt!
         Hunt!
130   *Hunt him!*

CLYTEMNESTRA:
You're preying on a dream, howling dogs,
hounding, hunting, chasing blood.
What are you doing? Wake up! Weariness will not win!
Sleep shall not rob your memories of my pain.
My scorn will stab your hearts,   135
a spur to prick the conscience of the just.
Let him feel the blast of your reeking, bloody breath,
bleed him dry and burn him in your stomach's fire.
On again! Hunt him down! Waste him away!

CHORUS:
Awake!
    Awake!
        All awake!   140
Shake off sleep.
        Up, up on your feet.
Seek out the truth of the dream.

(*Exit Clytemnestra through the doors*)

(*Enter chorus one by one from the doors into the orchestra*)

[Strophe 1]

No! No! Sisters we have been wronged!

All my work—all our work, for nothing! Nothing!

No! No! I can't bear the pain, it hurts! It hurts!   145

Unbearable pain!

Our prey has slipped the net, our victim has fled.

Sleep has beaten me, the hunt is lost.

[Antistrophe 1]

Son of Zeus, you are a thief!
The youth galloped past the ancient spirits,   150
but your sacred suppliant is a godless man,
a curse to those that raised him.

You have stolen the mother-killer, you, a god!
How can this be justice?

[Strophe 2]

155   *The charge was leveled in my dream,*
        it lashed me like a chariot whip
        held hard and strong,
        it stung my mind, it thrashed my heart.

160   *I felt the harsh crack and the searing smart*
        of the floggers punishing scourge.

[Antistrophe 2]

These new gods, this is how they behave,
their power exceeds the bounds of justice.
Their thrones are drenched in blood,
165   *soaked from head to foot.*

I see the center-stone stained,
defiled, accursed, grim with gore.

[Strophe 3]

The prophet has fouled his hearth and home,
sullied his own sanctuary, he invited it,
170   *he encouraged it.*

He flouts the law, puts men before gods,
he destroys the ancient lot of Destiny.

[Antistrophe 3]

He has wounded us, but the man will not escape,
175   *he can run to the ends of the earth, he'll never be free.*

He'll take the mark of murder to his grave,
more blood will come, on his own head be it.

        (Enter Apollo from the doors)

177: Apollo may have entered on the roof of the scene building.

APOLLO:
Out I say! Get away from my house!
leave the prophetic chamber,   180
or feel the fangs of my winged serpents
flashing from my gold-stringed bow.
I'll pierce your guts, and you'll spew the black blood
and scum sucked from men, and choke on the putrid clots.
There is no place for you in this house, you have no right
   here.   185
You belong where justice slaughters men for their crimes,
where heads are cut off and eyes gouged out,
where a man's seed is killed by castration
and young boys are mutilated, their bull-spirits crushed.
Go, follow the stonings, hear the tortured cries of men,   190
hover by the carcasses, staked out, driven through, impaled.
You crave your ghastly feast and the gods despise you.
Look at you! You are betrayed by your hideous shape,
you should cower in a cave, the carrion of a lion
gorged with blood. Never smear your filth on my shrine.   195
Get out! Out, you headless herd, there's not a god
in heaven who would deign to be your shepherd.

CHORUS:
Lord Apollo, listen, it is our turn to speak.
You are not merely an accessory to this crime,
it was all your doing, you bear the blame.   200

APOLLO:
How? Tell me that, nothing more.

CHORUS:
Your oracle told the outcast to kill his mother.

APOLLO:
My oracle told him to exact revenge for his father, what of it?

CHORUS:
You offered to shelter him, the blood still on his hands.

191: The audience of the *Oresteia* would have associated these punishments with the practices of the Persians and other Eastern "barbarians."

APOLLO:

205   I told him to come to my house as a suppliant.

CHORUS:

But we brought him here and now you malign us.

APOLLO:

You should not come anywhere near my house.

CHORUS:

But it is our responsibility, it is our place.

APOLLO:

By what authority? Please proclaim your ancient prerogative.

CHORUS:

210   We drive mother-killers from their homes.

APOLLO:

And what do you do when a wife kills her husband?

CHORUS:

Then the killer would not be spilling kindred blood.

APOLLO:

Then you demean and dishonor
the marriage vows of Hera Fulfiller and Zeus.
215   Your statement discards Aphrodite to disgrace,
she, who seals the most cherished of mortal bonds.
The marriage of a man and woman is set by Destiny,
it is mightier than the oath and defended by Justice.
If you are prepared to allow murder in marriage,
220   and take no vengeance nor inflict your wrath,
then this manhunt of Orestes cannot be just.
I see that the one issue inflames your hearts,
but clearly for the other, you are unwilling to act.

214: Hera was the daughter of Cronus and wife of Zeus and is invoked here in her guise of goddess of marriage. The union of Zeus and Hera was considered the first and foremost of all marriages.

215: The goddess of sexual love and reproduction.

I say the goddess Athena should preside over this case.

CHORUS:
We will never let that man be free, never!   225

APOLLO:
Well, chase him then, and suffer the consequences.

CHORUS:
I will not allow you to argue away our authority.

APOLLO:
Authority? If it was offered to me I would refuse it.

CHORUS:
Of course, for you are a mighty god enthroned by Zeus,
but we are forced on by the shedding of mother blood,   230
and Justice is best served by hunting the killer down.

   (Exit Furies through the stage left wing)

APOLLO:
He is in my sacred trust and I will protect him.
Gods and men fear nothing more than the rage
of a scorned suppliant denied his mercy.

   (Exit Apollo through the doors)

SCENE 2: *Athens, at the foot of Athena's statue before her temple.*

   *(Enter Orestes from the stage left wing into the orchestra; he
   falls at the altar.)*

ORESTES:
Lady Athena, I have come at the command of Apollo,   235
greet this outcast with kind good grace.

235: It is not known how this scene change was marked. It may have
been achieved simply with the removal of the chorus, a rare occurrence
in tragedy, followed by the arrival of Orestes at the theatre altar in the
center of the orchestra. Because the text has made it clear that Orestes
must journey to Athens and Orestes himself opens the scene with an
appeal to Athena, it would not have been necessary to set an actual representation of Athena's statue on stage.

I am not an untouchable, my hands are clean,
I am like a dulled blade, blunted in faraway homes,
beaten and battered on the roads of men.
240   I traveled the earth and spanned the seas,
following the oracle, the word of Apollo,
heading for your house, goddess, for your idol.
Now I'm here, I'll watch and wait for the final
      judgment.

(Enter the Furies from the stage left wing)

CHORUS:
We have him! Look, the man-tracks, a fresh trail,
245   follow the silent evidence, it points the way.
Hound him, hunt him like a wounded fawn,
track the trace of a blood-splattered scent.
This deadly work, no man could bear it, gasping,
lung-splitting labor, sweeping across the earth,
250   skimming the seas in wingless flight,
swifter than a ship, bearing down on our prey.
He is here, skulking somewhere near,
I smell the welcome stench of human blood.

Look! Look!
255   *Look everywhere!*
The mother-killer must not escape, he must be punished.

(The Furies see Orestes.)

There he is! He's taken sanctuary!
He's clinging to the idol of the goddess!
260   *He wants to wipe his hands clean with a trial!*
No! He has spilled his mother's blood!
It is done, drained away, it can't come back!
Swallowed by the earth, gone forever!
Blood must pay for blood!

(To Orestes)

                              We will drink
265   *the thick, red liquid libation of your limbs*

and quench our thirst with a sickening toast.
We will bleed you dry then banish you below.
We'll see you in hell, one more for the wicked,
with the men who sinned against gods, guests,
and their own dear parents.   270
You'll suffer the pain that Justice ordains.
Mighty Hades balances the human ledger,
his final reckoning holds mortals to account,
deep in the depths of the earth everything
is remembered and etched on his mind.   275

ORESTES:

Evil has educated me. I have come to understand
many things, I know when to speak
and when to stay silent, and in this case
a wise teacher has told me to voice my case.
The blood on my hands has been worn to sleep,   280
the mark of mother-killing has been washed out.
The fresh stain was purged before Apollo's hearth,
cleansed by the blood of slaughtered swine.
It would take too long to tell you of all the homes
that sheltered me and yet were never tainted.   285
All things age and time can cleanse everything.
Now my pure and pious lips call on Athena,
queen of this country, to come to my aid.
Win without the spear, me, my country,
and all my Argive people, forevermore   290
trusted allies and confederates true.
She will come from the shores of Africa,
by the waters of Triton that bore her,
to lead the charge or to stand in defense,

272: The son of Cronus and Rhea; brother of Zeus and god of the underworld.

283: The blood of a freshly slaughtered piglet was used as part of the ritual purification of a killer.

293: Lake Tritonis in Libya, North Africa, was said to be the birthplace of Athena.

295   she will enter the fight to rescue an ally.   ·
       She'll come striding the monstrous battleground,
       surveying the field like a bold man of war.
       I know she can hear me, I know she can save me.

CHORUS:
       There is no salvation, not from Apollo, nor Athena.
300   You will be cast out, adrift, abandoned,
       your tortured mind will never know happiness,
       you'll be food for fiends, a blood-sucked shadow.
       You refuse to answer? You spit on our words?
       You are our sacrifice fatted for the feast,
305   you'll not be slashed at the altar, we'll eat you alive!
       Now hear our song, our spellbinding song.

                              [Prelude]

       Join our binding dance
       the malignant music
       unfolding the terror.
310   *Hear our share*
       in the life of man,
       for we are just and true.
       Hold up clean hands
       and clear wrath's trail,
315   *pass life free from harm.*
       Should you, like him, stray to sin
       and hide your murderous hands,
       then we bear witness for the dead.
       For bloodshed must be revenged,
320   *and we pursue it to the very end.*

296: This is the Phlegrean plain, located in Macedonia, where the
Olympian gods were said to have fought the race of giants for su-
premacy over the earth. This Gigantomachy was a popular theme in
Greek art and literature, representing the triumph of "civilization over
barbarianism."

307: The Furies sing their "binding song," a malicious incantation
meant to curse the victim and render him powerless.

[Strophe 1]

Mother who made me,
Mother Night hear me,
bred to avenge the sighted,
the blind, bred to avenge the dead.
Leto's child has stolen the hare,
Apollo tries to rob my rights,
we demand this sacrifice
payment for mother-blood shed.   325

[Refrain 1]

We sing for the victim
insanity's song,
delirious, demented,   330
the Furies' hymn,
spellbinding minds,
unstrung strains burning the brain.

[Antistrophe 1]

Our share of the thread
spun by the spirits of Destiny,   335
woven in permanent place.
We hunt down the mortal
compelled to kill kin,
hound him to hell,
down, down, deep in the earth,
he'll never be free, even in death.   340

[Refrain 1]

We sing for the victim

322: Leto was a Titan, the daughter of Coeus and Phoebe and the mother by Zeus of Apollo and Artemis. The female forces in the trilogy often use epithets that trace the maternal lineage of male gods and heroes (see *Agamemnon*, 1040).

335: In one mythological personification the force of Destiny was depicted as the three "Fates." These weaving female deities—Clotho, Lachesis, and Atropos—spun, allotted, and sheared the threads of human existence.

insanity's song:
delirious, demented,
the Furies' hymn:
345 *spellbinding minds,*
unstrung strains burning the brain.

[Strophe 2]

Our birthright, our share, ordained of old,
350 *untouched by the deathless gods.*
They never deign to sit at our feasts,
not for us the pure white robes,
they have no share in our dark rites.

[Refrain 2]

I reduce to ruin the House
355 *that rears the brood of Ares*
breeding kin killing kin.
Born of the blood, we hunt down
the killer, scorning his power,
casting bleak shadows of death.

[Antistrophe 2]

360 *We eagerly fulfill this obligation,*
absolving the gods from this care;
they need never hear these charges.
365 *Zeus detests our gruesome kind,*
and shuns us from his side.

[Strophe 3]

A man's esteem, the light of his life
can decay to disgrace once deep in the earth.
370 *The black-clad chorus closes around,*
feet pounding the furious dance.

[Refrain 3]

Leaping from the heights,
the hard, heavy downfall.
My foot stamps and cripples,

the straining runner is brought down,   375
crashing to ground, reduced by Ruin.

[Antistrophe 3]

He cannot see his downfall,
depravity drives him mad,
polluted mists cloud all reason.
Darkness hovers over his House,
a sigh of grief breathes the doom.   380

[Strophe 4]

And so it stands, this our craft,
fulfillment of the evil,
for remembrance is respect,   .
however much a man may beg.
The gods hate our gory share,   385
shunned in sunless grime.
Our rugged path is the only way
for both the living and the dead.

[Antistrophe 4]

What mortal man is not terrified,
gripped in fear and horror   390
to hear our sacred law
determined by Destiny's decree?
The gods yield this right,
it is our age-old prerogative,
and though we dwell in sunless depths   395
our underworld power stands respected.

(Enter Athena from the doors)

ATHENA:
I heard a far cry for help from Scamander's

398: Because the scene building has been established as Athena's temple in Athens, it seems logical that the goddess would enter via the
doors. This would also place her in the most dominant position on
stage. Some have envisioned her entrance by foot from the wings or
riding on a chariot into the orchestra.

shores, where I claimed the land bestowed
by the warriors and chiefs of Greece.
400   The greatest share of the spear-won spoils,
branch and root, are mine for all time,
the choicest prize for Theseus' sons.
I have come stepping swiftly, stridently
my flailing Aegis whirling me wingless.
405   [yoking young steeds to my chariot.]
I see new visitors have come to my land,
an astounding sight, but I am not afraid.
Who or what are you? I speak to you all,
both the stranger crouched at my statue,
and you, inhuman grotesque creatures
410   fatherless by birth, and reared
by no goddesses known to the gods.
But prejudice is slander to the innocent,
and Justice should always be impartial.

CHORUS:
415   Daughter of Zeus, I will explain,
we are the eternal children of Night,
the curses that dwell deep in the earth.

ATHENA:
I know of your kind, I have heard your name.

398: This may be a reference to the Athenian colony at Sigeum in the
Troas. This was the first Athenian overseas possession and the source of
an ownership dispute between Athens and the island of Mytilene in the
late sixth century.

402: Theseus was the legendary king and hero of Athens, famous for
his defeat of the Cretan Minotaur but also credited with purging Attica
of monsters and unifying the region politically. To the Athenian of the
mid-fifth century he civilized Athens, planted the seeds of democracy,
and was a symbol of their city's greatness.

404: This was Athena's breastplate, worn around her neck with the
head of Medusa at its center.

405: This line may be a later interpolation.

CHORUS:
> And you will soon hear of our authority.

ATHENA:
> If you state your case clearly, I will learn it.   *420*

CHORUS:
> We drive murderers from their homes.

ATHENA:
> And where does this murder-hunt end?

CHORUS:
> In a place that has never known joy.

ATHENA:
> Is this your fugitive, are you hunting him?

CHORUS:
> Yes, he saw fit to murder his mother.   *425*

ATHENA:
> Was he forced? Did he fear the anger of another?

CHORUS:
> What could goad a man to kill his own mother?

ATHENA:
> There are two sides to this, it is only half-heard.

CHORUS:
> But he will not swear the oath of innocence, nor accept our
> oath of his guilt.

ATHENA:
> So you would rather be called just than act justly?   *430*

429: Athenian legal custom required the defendant to swear innocence
and the prosecutor to swear that he believed the defendant to be guilty.
If either party refused this oath, then the case was forfeited by default.
Orestes' situation is not quite so clearcut, and Athena recognizes this.

CHORUS:
What do you mean? You are wise, teach us.

ATHENA:
An oath must never triumph over Justice.

CHORUS:
Then question him, you judge the justice.

ATHENA:
Will you give the final say in this case to me?

CHORUS:
435 Yes, respect from you makes our respect due.

ATHENA:
Stranger, it is your turn to speak, to answer these charges.
Tell me where you are from, your family and your troubles,
then make your defense against these claims.
If it is your belief in Justice that has you huddling at my
hearth,
440 clutching my statue, then your rights will be respected
and held sacred as a suppliant like Ixion before you.
Now address these issues and answer them clearly.

ORESTES:
Lady Athena, first of all please allow me to dispel
a misgiving I have over what you have just said to me.
445 I am not a suppliant, and it is not because my hands
are stained that I sit here at the foot of your image.
I have powerful proof that I am speaking the truth.
Divine law holds that a murderer must not speak
until a man who can perform the cleansing rite
450 sprinkles him with the blood of a suckling beast.
Also, I have long since been purged by the sacrifices

441: Ixion was the mythical king of Thessaly and the first mortal murderer. He was said to have killed his father and was purified by Zeus.
But he abused heaven's hospitality and was punished by being bound
to a wheel of fire, spinning in eternity.

and lustral waters of all the homes that took me in.
So you see, the pollution must not be considered.
You will soon recognize my lineage.
I am an Argive, and you know my father well,   455
Agamemnon, the man who marshaled the fleet
and with your help, crushed the city of Troy.
Returning home he died a miserable death,
hacked down by my foul-minded mother,
shrouded in the intricate covert net,   460
the witness of the murder in the bath.
I was in exile then, but when I returned
I killed the woman who bore me. I do not deny it.
It was revenge for the murder of my beloved father.
Apollo was my accomplice, he shares the charge,   465
he lashed me with threats of heartwrenching pains
if I did not take action against the guilty ones.
You judge if I was just or not. I have made my case.
Whatever you decide, I will accept your verdict.

ATHENA:
This matter is too great to be decided by a mortal.   470
It is not even appropriate that I preside over
a murder trial that inflames such furious rage.
You have been tamed by the rites, fully cleansed
and have sought rightful sanctuary at my house.

  (Indicating the Furies)

But Destiny has allotted their place, and it cannot   475
simply be dismissed, for if they were defeated
the wound of their resentment would seep malignant poison,
cursing the earth with an insufferable, perpetual plague.
So stands the case. Do I let you stay, or send you away?
An arduous decision, as either way will provoke divine wrath. 480
Because this case has become my responsibility
I will appoint the exemplary men of my city
as magistrates over murder, bound by a solemn oath,
for now and for ever, to serve this sacred court.

480: Rejecting a suppliant was a crime even for gods, but Athena recognizes the right of the Furies to avenge familial murder.

485   Summon your witnesses and gather your evidence,
         prepare your sworn testimonies to support your cases.
         I will select the finest of my citizens
         who will strive to return an honest verdict,
         uphold their pledge, and deliberate with judicial minds.

                    (*Exit Athena through the doors*)

                         [Strophe 1]

CHORUS:
490   *Catastrophe! Ancient*
         mandates will be usurped
         should the corrupt plea
         of the mother-killer prevail.
         His crime will unite all mankind
495   *in anarchy and lawlessness,*
         down through the generations,
         children will be free to harm parents,
         the fatal lesions tearing true.

                         [Antistrophe 1]

         We are the Furies, sentinels,
500   *but no longer will we keep watch*
         and rage against the depraved.
         We will abandon all mankind.
         Let slip the impending doom.
505   *Let man appeal to man for heaven's help*
         and prophesy his neighbor's troubles.
         Let him tell when the pain will ease and cease,
         and offer the poor fool his ineffective cure.

                         [Strophe 2]

         Now no one may call on us
         when disaster rains down.
510   *Yet they will clamor to cry,*
         "Justice, where are you!
         Sovereign Furies!"
         The tormented father,
         the mother just wronged,

they will bemoan and wail   515
the collapse of the house of Justice.

[Antistrophe 2]

Fear has its place, it can be good,
it stands sentinel,
the watchman of the mind.
It can be beneficial   520
to suffer into sanity.
How can the man
or city that has no fear
to nourish the heart
ever have respect for Justice?   525

[Strophe 3]

Not a life of anarchy
nor the rule of tyranny.
Take the middle way endowed by gods
whatever course they sway.   530
In accord we sing measured words:
Outrage is Impiety's true child,
only a healthy mind provides   535
the good fortune so cherished,
the passion of all men's prayers.

[Antistrophe 3]

Know this now, know it all.
Respect Justice, never kick away
her altar for the glimpse of wealth.   540
The disgrace will be avenged,
for the end remains ordained.
Hold parents in the high esteem,   545
grace the sacred guest,
keep your house hospitable,
honor strangers with your good fortune.

534: This is *hubris* (outrage), shameful behavior that goes against religious, moral, and social values.

[Strophe 4]

550   *Freely embrace Justice*
         and you will surely prosper,
         you will never know destruction.
         The insolent violator heaping high
         his unjust haul, hoarding his vicious
555   *payload, will soon enough strike his sails*
         as his yardarm cracks and shatters,
         against the blasts of suffering's storm.

[Antistrophe 4]

         His cries for help fall on deaf ears
         as he founders in the whirling currents.
560   *The spirits see and mock the brazen man*
         who once boasted this could never be.
         Helplessly drowning in a sea of sorrows,
         his fortune submerged in a surge of woes,
         wrecked upon the reef of Justice.
565   *He is lost, unwept, unseen.*

SCENE 3: *The hill of Ares (Areopagus) in Athens.*

   (Enter Athena from the doors)

ATHENA:
   Herald, summon the people to their places,
   raise the Tyrrhenian war trumpet,
   fill its bronze with mortal breath,
   sound the piercing cry to call the people.

566: There was probably no actual scenery change or additional prop setting here, apart from the placing of the voting urns by the arriving jurors. The words of Athena on her exit and entrance and the intervening choral ode would have been sufficient to mark the change of location. Orestes could then stay by the altar with perhaps his mask turned away from the audience to place the dramatic focus on the chorus.

567: The Etruscans of central Italy. According to legend they invented the trumpet.

(Enter ten Athenian elders from the stage right wing into the orchestra. They set two large voting urns.)

Be silent as the court convenes,   570
the city will learn my eternal laws,
the litigants will receive a fair trial
and hear a prudent judgment.

(Enter Apollo on the roof)

Lord Apollo, you have your own jurisdiction;
tell me, how you are involved in this case?   575

APOLLO:
I have come to testify under the law.
This man is my suppliant and sought sanctuary
at my hearth, I purged him of his blood-guilt.
I stand as his advocate and share the blame
for the murder of his mother. I ask you   580
to decide this case. I seek your judgment.

ATHENA:
Begin the proceedings.

(To the Furies)

Make your case.
The prosecution will present its arguments first.
Explain your accusations and set out your charges.

CHORUS:
Although we are many, we will be brief,   585

570: The exact number of jurors is not completely clear from the text. The series of ten couplets at 711ff. suggest a group of ten.

574: It is difficult to pin down Apollo's movements in this scene. His sudden entrance and departure work well on the roof of the scene building, which also creates a spatial opposition between the chthonic Furies in the orchestra and Olympian Apollo high on the roof. It would be appropriate for Athena as mediator to be on stage in the central position.

(To Orestes)

Answer our questions point for point.
Tell us first, did you kill your mother?

ORESTES:
I killed her, I do not deny it. .

CHORUS:
There! The first of three falls.

ORESTES:
You boast before the bout is over. I am not yet down for the
590   count.

CHORUS:
Will you tell us how you killed her?

ORESTES:
I held my sword at her neck and slit her throat.

CHORUS:
Who persuaded you to do this, who advised it?

ORESTES:
It was the god's word, he will testify to that.

CHORUS:
595   The prophet guided you to kill your own mother?

ORESTES:
Yes, and as yet I have no regrets.

CHORUS:
You will, when the verdict places you in our grasp.

ORESTES:
I have faith in my father, help from beyond the grave.

CHORUS:
You trust the dead? You? The mother-killer!

ORESTES:

Yes, I killed her, because she was tainted with two crimes. 600

CHORUS:

How? Explain that to the jury.

ORESTES:

She murdered her husband and she murdered my father.

CHORUS:

But she was absolved by her death, while you still live.

ORESTES:

Then why did you not drive her out when she was alive?

CHORUS:

She was not of the same blood as the man she murdered. 605

ORESTES:

So do I share my mother's blood?

CHORUS:

You butcher! You grew in her womb, how can you disown
the bond of blood between mother and child?

ORESTES:

Apollo guide me now, stand as my witness,
was Justice with me when I struck her down? 610
The deed was done, I did it, I do not deny it.
Consider the bloodshed and give your decision,
they must hear my side of this case, was I just?

APOLLO:

I say to you, and to this great court of Athena,
that he was just. I am the seer and I speak the truth. 615
No man, woman, or city has ever heard a word
from my seat of prophecy that was not
ordained by Zeus, the Olympian father.
Understand the force behind this just plea
and be sure you heed the will of my father, 620
for no oath can surpass the power of Zeus.

CHORUS:
Zeus? Are you saying Zeus gave you this oracle?
That he told Orestes to seek revenge for his father
by disregarding the honor he owed his mother?

APOLLO:
625   Clearly there is no comparison. He was avenging the death
of a nobleman sceptered with Zeus-given honor.
The man was struck down by a woman, but not in battle
by the furious flight of an Amazon's arrow.
No, you will hear how he died, Athena,
630   as will the jury who will decide the verdict.
He returned from the long war and in the balance
he had done well, and she welcomed him with kindness.
As he stepped from the bath, at the very edge,
she threw that shroud around him, tangling him
635   in the endless, intricate fabric—and then she struck.
I have told you how this awe-inspiring man,
the First Sea Lord of the fleet, met his end.
It enrages the people to hear what she did,
as it should enrage you judges deciding this case.

CHORUS:
640   You say that Zeus has higher regard for a father's destiny,
and yet he placed his own father, old Cronus, in chains.
This seems to contradict your argument,
I call on the jurors to witness this.

APOLLO:
You repulsive hags! The gods detest you!
645   Chains can be broken, there is a remedy
and countless ways to be set free.
But once the dust has soaked up a man's blood
he is gone forever, nothing can bring him back.
Zeus has provided no magic charm for that,
650   though he has the power to change the course
of everything, breathlessly, at his whim.

641: Cronus was overthrown by Zeus and held in chains deep beneath
the earth in Tartarus.

CHORUS:
　　Look at how you justify his defense!
　　He spilled his own mother's blood on the ground,
　　and you would have him home in Argos at his father's house?
　　Tell me, what communal altars could he worship at?　　　655
　　What clan could ever anoint and admit him?

APOLLO:
　　Then learn the truth, the one named mother
　　is not the child's true parent but the nurturer
　　of the newly sown seed. Man mounts to create life,
　　whereas woman is a stranger fostering a stranger,　　　660
　　nourishing the young, unless a god blights the birth.
　　I have proof that there can be a father without a mother,
　　proof that what I say is true,
　　there stands your witness:

　　　　(Indicating Athena)

　　　　　　　　　　The child of Zeus.
　　She never grew in the darkness of a womb,　　　665
　　and no goddess could have borne such a child.

　　Athena, in all things I will do my utmost
　　to help your city and its people achieve greatness.
　　I sent this man to your house and hearth
　　that you may be bound in trust for all time　　　670
　　and that you would inherit a new ally, goddess.
　　Both he and his descendants true to you for ever,
　　the generations bonded in a covenant of faith.

ATHENA:
　　Have we heard enough? May I call on the jury
　　to deliberate and deliver their truthful verdict?　　　675

APOLLO:
　　We have shot all our defensive bolts.
　　I stay only to hear the decision in this dispute.

665: Athena was born fully grown from the head of Zeus.

ATHENA:
Very well,

(*To the Furies*)

and how can I best appease you?

CHORUS:
You have heard what you have heard, may the jury search
680   their hearts and respect their oath as they cast their votes.

ATHENA:
Now hear my decree, people of Athens.
You are the first to judge a case of bloodshed.
And from this time on, the race of Aegeus
will forever uphold this judicial assembly.
685   When the Amazon warrior women invaded,
they pitched their camp on this rock of Ares.
Those foes of Theseus forced into your city and raised
their towering battlements that dwarfed your walls.
They dedicated this place for the war god,
690   and on this hill of Ares I will found my court.
From this rock shall come the respect to inspire
my citizens and the fear to restrain injustice,
constant through every long night and each bright day.
But the citizens must uphold the law
695   and there can be no deviation, for pure water
can never be drawn once the well has been fouled.
There will be no anarchy, nor the rule of tyranny.
Citizens, embrace the middle way, but never banish fear,
for the mortal who has no fear can never know Justice.

684: Originally the meeting place for the Aristocratic council that heard
cases pertaining to the welfare of the state. In 462/1 B.C.E., Ephialtes
may have enacted reforms that stripped this power from the Aereopa-
gus and redistributed it to the developing citizen government. The
power to try cases of homicide was left in place, and this may be an allusion to this recent controversial political activity.

688: The Amazons were a legendary tribe of warrior women from Asia
Minor who had invaded Athens and made their encampment on the
Areopagus.

You must respect this court and you must fear it, 700
it is your best defense, for the stronger the bulwark,
the safer the city, and men will never know a city stronger,
whether it lies in the land of Pelops or in Scythian hills.
This tribunal will be untouchable, and not corrupt,
distinguished, but swift to act, the watchtower 705
of our country, the sentinel of safe, sound sleep.
I dedicate this address to my people, both now
and in the time to come. Let each man stand
and cast his ballot so we may decide this case,
and remember always to respect your oath. 710

(One by one, the ten jurors cast their votes.)

CHORUS:
I warn you, together we could curse your earth.
It would be wise not to dishonor us.

APOLLO:
And I remind you to heed my oracles, the word of Zeus;
do not deprive them of bearing their fruit.

CHORUS:
You are meddling in matters of blood, and it is not your place. 715
Your house will be unclean and your oracles tainted.

APOLLO:
So was Zeus mistaken when he offered sanctuary
to Ixion, the very first man to commit a murder?

CHORUS:
So you say, but if we do not receive some justice,
we will curse this land for the rest of time. 720

APOLLO:
You are a disgrace to the gods, young and old alike.
I will win, I will defeat you.

711: The following ten couplets that make up the exchange between
Apollo and the Furies may have accompanied each of the votes cast by
the ten jurors.

CHORUS:
Just like the time you interfered in the House of Pheres
and persuaded the spirits of Destiny to free a mortal from
    death.

APOLLO:
725   How can it not be just to aid the faithful man
especially in his time of greatest trouble?

CHORUS:
You obliterated age-old precedents,
you beguiled the ancient goddesses with wine.

APOLLO:
Soon enough you will lose this trial.
730   Spit your poison at your enemies. It will do them no harm.

CHORUS:
This youth rides roughshod over his elders,
but we will wait to hear the verdict
and then decide if this city will incur our wrath.

ATHENA:
Now my task is to make the last judgment,
735   and I cast my vote for Orestes.
I was born of no mother, and I defer to the male
in all things with all my heart, except for marriage,
as I will always be the child of my father.
Thus, I cannot give precedence to the woman's death:
740   she murdered her husband, the guardian of the House;
if the vote is split Orestes will be the winner.
Now the jury foremen will proceed with the count,
quickly, turn out the urns and tally the votes.

(The urns are emptied and the votes counted.)

723: This is a reference to Admetus, who had been saved from death by
Apollo after the god had persuaded the spirits of Destiny to take a re-
placement victim. This turned out to be Admetus' wife Alcestis, who
was eventually saved by Persephone, or in some versions by Heracles.

ORESTES:
   Apollo, lord of the light, what will be decided?

CHORUS:
   Dark Mother Night, are you watching?   745

ORESTES:
   Is it death at the end of a rope, or will I see the light of life?

CHORUS:
   Is it the end for us or a new sanction of our authority?

APOLLO:
   The ballots are out, make a careful count, be fair,
   have respect for Justice as you divide the votes.
   An ill-judged verdict could cause great harm,   750
   and a single vote can restore a mighty House.

ATHENA:
   Each side has received the same number of votes.
   This man is acquitted of the charge of murder.

ORESTES:
   Athena, you have saved my House!
   I was denied the land of my fathers,   755
   but you have restored me to my home.
   The Greeks will say, "The man is Argive again.
   He holds his father's House by the grace of Athena
   and Apollo, ordained by the Savior, Zeus the Third."
   Zeus marked the death of my father and saved   760
   me from the litigants sent by my mother.
   And as I leave for home I will make a great oath.
   I swear to you, your land and your people,
   that for the rest of time, no helmsman guiding
   my country will ever raise a spear against you,   765
   or march in force to do battle against this land.
   I will protect this promise from beyond my grave

766: This may be an illusion to the recent treaty with Argos of 461
B.C.E., which created a political alliance to counter Spartan power.

and will rise up and punish the oathbreaker.
I will slow their march to a disastrous crawl,
770   crush their spirits with the birds of ill omen,
force them down the path of penance and regret.
Yet if they respect this oath and forever honor
this city of Athena with their confederate spears,
I will bless them with good will and eternal kindness.
775   So farewell to you and the people of your city,
may your bouts be won, and your holds be strong,
may the safety of our spears bring victorious years.

> (*Exit Orestes through the stage left wing. Exit Apollo from the
> roof*)

[Strophe 1]

CHORUS:
> *You young gods have ridden roughshod over*
> *the ancient ways, wrenched them from our grasp.*
780   > *We are dishonored and dejected,*
> *and our anger rises to ravage the land.*
> *Venom boiled from grief,*
> *seeping from seething hearts,*
> *poison oozing on the earth,*
> *sterile, stagnant pestilence*
785   > *polluting the ground. Oh Justice! Justice!*
> *Mortal infection will disease this place.*
> *Ai, I lament, what will I do?*
> *Scorned by the people,*
> *unbearable mockery!*
790   > *Ill-fated daughters of Night*
> *you are cast out,*
> *you are disgraced!*

ATHENA:
Be persuaded not to bear this burden of grief.
795   You were not defeated, the votes were even,
it was an honest verdict, there is no disgrace.
We heard the clear testimony of Zeus,
and it said that Orestes should not suffer,
it was evidenced by the prophet-god himself.

Now you threaten this land with your terrible wrath,　　　　*800*
but curb your anger, do not poison the soil
by smearing your demonic venom, and ploughing
this fecund earth into a barren wasteland.
I swear by Justice that you will receive your due respect.
I will give you a shrine of the earth in this righteous land　　*805*
and seat you on gleaming thrones beside an altar,
where my citizens will worship you with honor.

[Antistrophe 1]

CHORUS:
You young gods have ridden roughshod over
the ancient ways, wrenched them from our grasp.
We are dishonored, and dejected,　　　　*810*
and our anger rises to ravage the land.
Venom boiled from grief,
seeping from the seething hearts,
poison oozing on the earth,
sterile, stagnant pestilence
polluting the ground. Oh Justice! Justice!　　　　*815*
Mortal infection will disease this place.
Ai, I lament, what will I do?
Scorned by the people,
unbearable mockery!
Ill-fated daughters of Night　　　　*820*
you are cast out,
you are disgraced!

ATHENA:
You are not disgraced, control your rage,
you are gods, do not devastate mortal land.　　　　*825*
I put my trust in Zeus, it goes without saying,
and I am the only other god who holds the key
to the treasury where he stores the thunderbolts.
But they are not needed, let me persuade you instead:
don't let your malicious tongues lash this land　　　　*830*
and curse the bounteous earth with blight.
Soothe to sleep your dark tide of bitter fury,
for you will be revered in honor and live here with me.
This magnificent city will sacrifice the first rites

835   of birth and marriage to you forevermore.
      I know you will come to bless these words.

[Strophe 2]

CHORUS:
     I must suffer this? Ancient wisdom
     buried deep down under this land,
     dishonored and despised!
840   *All is rage, breathe the fury!*
     Oh the fury!
     Oh!
     Ah, the pain! stabbing, side-splitting pain!
     Ai, Mother Night!
845   *Honors gone, stripped away,*
     the cheating gods have left us nothing!

ATHENA:
     I will indulge your anger because you are my elders
     and in this respect you possess greater wisdom.
850   But Zeus has made my mind for good,
     and I know that if you leave for foreign lands
     I promise your hearts will long for Athens.
     Here the passage of time will lead to honor,
     my people will enshrine you on stately thrones
855   next to the house of Erechtheus, and a sacred
     procession of men and women will grace you
     with gifts unsurpassed in the mortal realm.
     Leave your gory grindstones that whet the appetite
     for blood, and sicken the stomachs of the young
860   with intoxicating ferocity and bloodthirsty rage.
     The gamecock's violent heart will never beat
     in their breasts, and throb to the pulse of Ares,
     that internal hemorrhage that bleeds civil war.
     Let our battles be abroad and let them come,
865   they will quench our thirst for fame and glory.

855: Erechtheus was legendary king of Athens who had a shrine on the
Acropolis. He was said to have been born from the Earth and raised by
Athena.

I damn the bird that fights its own and fouls the nest.
This is the choice I offer, you must decide.
Do good, gain goodness, receive goodly honors,
and take your share of this land beloved by gods.

[Antistrophe 2]

CHORUS:
I must suffer this? Ancient wisdom   870
buried deep down under this land,
dishonored and despised!
All is rage, breathe the fury!
Oh the fury!
Oh!   875
Ah, the pain! stabbing, side-splitting pain!
Ai, Mother Night!
Honors gone, stripped away,
the cheating gods leave us nothing!   880

ATHENA:
I will not tire of telling you the benefits I offer,
I will not let you ancient goddesses claim
that a younger god and her city's people
banished you, branded as outcasts.
If you have any respect for the power of Persuasion   885
let my words soothe and enchant you
to decide to stay. But if you do choose to leave,
it would be unjust to bring down your anger,
rage, and destruction upon these people,
for I have offered you a share in this land,   890
bestowed by Justice with eternal honor.

CHORUS:
Lady Athena, where is the place that will be mine?

ATHENA:
It is a place free from pain and suffering. Will you accept it?

CHORUS:
And if I do, what honors await me?

ATHENA:
895   No house will prosper without your help.

CHORUS:
        And you would really give me that power?

ATHENA:
        I will flourish the fortune of all your worshipers.

CHORUS:
        And will you promise this for all eternity?

ATHENA:
        Yes, I do not promise what I cannot fulfill.

CHORUS:
900   Your charms are working, the rage is subsiding.

ATHENA:
        Then live beneath this earth befriended by my
            people.

CHORUS:
        What song would you have me sing for this land?

ATHENA:
        Nothing discordant with our mutual victory,
        a blessing reaped from the earth, swept by the sea,
905   breathed on the wind down from the sky, brushing
        the land with balmy breezes touched by the sun.
        Then the fruits of the earth and plentiful herds
        will flourish for my people, an everlasting harvest,
        conserving the human seed, sowing new life,
910   cultivating the pious to make the righteous thrive.
        I grow good men like the caring gardener
        protecting this noble strain from the blight of sorrow.
        You could give such blessings as I tend to the arts
            of war
        the glorious challenge, for my quest is this city's
915   victorious pride of place, admired by all mankind.

[Strophe 1]

CHORUS:
> We accept a home in this land of Pallas.
> We will not dishonor a city ruled by Ares,
> defender of gods and Zeus Almighty.
> This sentinel of the sacred sites of Greece   920
> is beloved by all the immortals.
> Now for Athens we too will pray,
> and we foresee a future bright,
> the flourish of abundant life
> flowing out from a fecund land,   925
> sparkling in the sun's kind light.

ATHENA:
> With a mind for my people I do this,
> I root to our earth the mighty, the resolute,
> I settle these spirits here in our land,
> appointed to share the rule   930
> of the affairs of mortal man.
> Ignore their heavy hand and the blows
> rain down through life. Why?
> From where? Sins unredeemed,
> crimes of old will come before them,   935
> and for the loud boasts a silent ruin
> as hateful anger grinds to dust.

[Antistrophe 1]

CHORUS:
> We sing of the gifts we will give:
> no storm-winds will strike at your trees,
> no searing heat will ever burn   940
> scorching the earth, blistering your buds.

916: One of Athena's cult titles, possibly derived from the name of a legendary giant.

927: Athena recites anapests in harmony with choral verses, in contrast to the competing styles used by Clytemnestra and the chorus at *Agamemnon* 1407–1576.

We will banish the baneful blights
that once condemned the crops to death.
Let Pan bless all your flocks with twins,
at lambing time, born fit and strong.
945   May the earth herself give birth
to Hermes' horde of buried wealth,
Fortune's bounty given by gods.

ATHENA:
Guardians of the city, do you hear
what they will bring to pass?
950   The gods above and those below
know the power of a Fury,
how they work their ways
and bring fulfillment to all mankind.
A celebration, a cause to rejoice,
955   or a life blinded by a flood of tears.

                              [Strophe 2]

CHORUS:
The murderous man-killing stroke
we forbid from taking young life,
so that now the lovely young girls
may come to know the marriage rites.
960   Grant this, you mighty gods,
grant this, sister Destiny,
daughters of Mother Night,
spirits of Justice and Right.
You have a share in every house,
965   you bear down on every season.
Justice is your communion,
you are honored by every god.

946: Hermes was said to guide mortals to hidden treasure. This could
be a reference to the rich silver mines of Attica at Laurium. A new vein
was discovered in 483 B.C.E., and this wealth contributed to the com-
missioning of the Athenian fleet that defeated the Persians at the battle
of Salamis in 480 B.C.E.

ATHENA:
   Your minds are for my people,
   the promise of your powers pleases me.
   When I faced your harsh rejections 970
   dear Persuasion watched over me,
   leading my lips, training my tongue.
   Zeus of Good Council prevailed,
   bringing a victory for both,
   for common good, forevermore. 975

[Antistrophe 2]

CHORUS:
   I pray that the clash of civil war,
   that unrelenting devastation,
   never rages across this land.
   Let dust not drink the citizen's blood, 980
   may slaughter not breed slaughter.
   No more blood-crazed retribution,
   for this city will never feed Ruin.
   Now let joy pay debts of joy,
   a commonwealth for friend and foe, 985
   one joint spirit shared by all,
   a cure for the sufferings of all mankind.

ATHENA:
   You see? They speak their minds,
   they have found the path of good.
   In these fearsome faces 990
   I see great gain for this city,
   kind minds for kind minds.
   Honor them forevermore
   and steer this land, our city,
   down the path of righteousness. 995

[Strophe 3]

CHORUS:
   Rejoice, rejoice for the fortune of Destiny.
   Rejoice people of this city,

> *placed so close to Zeus himself,*
> *cherished by Athena's great love.*
1000 > *As time goes, discretion comes,*
> *for you sit beneath Athena's wings*
> *and you will be admired by Zeus.*

> (*Enter a group of women from the stage right wing, carrying*
> *torches and folded crimson cloaks*)

ATHENA:
> *Rejoice with me, as I lead the way,*
> *lit by holy light, raised by loyal escorts.*
1005 > *Down to the sacred chamber, down beneath*
> *the earth blessed by solemn sacrifice.*
> *Here to stem the rise of destruction,*
> *here to grow great gain for the land,*
> *and here to sow the seeds of victory!*
1010 > *Citizens of Athens, sons of Cranaus,*
> *lead these sacred guests, lead the way.*
> *May the people bless them kindly*
> *for the great good blessings that they bring.*

[Antistrophe 3]

CHORUS:
> *Rejoice, rejoice again for the city!*
1015 > *Rejoice, let it ring out aloud!*

1003: The trilogy closes with a sacred procession escorting the Furies (who have now become *Eumenides*, "Kindly Ones") to their new sanctuary in the city of Athens.

1005: There was a shrine to the Furies in their guise as the *Semnai* ("awesome ones") near the base of the Areopagus at the entrance to a deep cavern.

1010: A legendary early king of Athens. His name means "the rocky one."

1011: Athens allowed a large population of resident aliens called *Metics* to live and work in its territory. This unusually liberal approach to outsiders allowed arts, crafts, and trade to flourish. The Metics were given certain non-voting rights under the law.

All those who inhabit here,
both the divine and the mortal,
twin powers of Athena's land,
hold us guests in high esteem
and let good fortune bless your lives.   1020

ATHENA:
I thank you for your prayers and the vows you make
as I escort you by the gleaming light of brilliant torches
to your new home deep beneath this earth.
Go with my women, the sentinels of my shrine,
come to the core of the city, the heart of Athens,   1025
as this glorious procession ascends the rock of Theseus.
Come children, women and venerable ladies,
clothe them in robes of honor steeped in crimson,
lead on the light, burn high the torches.
This communion of kindness shining on our land   1030
will reap an eternal harvest of great, good men.

(The Furies are covered in crimson cloaks and escorted in
procession out of the orchestra through the stage right wing as
the women sing, leading the way.)

[Strophe 1]

WOMEN:
On, on to your home, mighty, glorious,
childless children of Night, our kind escort.
Sing the blessing song, people of this land.   1035

[Antistrophe 1]

Deep, deep down in the earth's ancient cavern
we sacrifice, we honor and worship.
Sing the blessing song, people gathered here.

1028: The Panathenaea procession in honor of Athena included a con-
tingent of Metics who wore crimson tunics. The symbolism of crimson
fabric, which had theatrically dominated key scenes of both *Agamemnon* (905–974) and *The Libation Bearers* (980–1006), is repeated here.

[Strophe 2]

1040   *Your gentle minds will be kind to our land.*
        Come now you solemn goddesses, follow
        in delight the way of the torchlight's flame.
        Raise the hallowed cry, join our blessing our song!

[Antistrophe 2]

        The peace for both citizen and settler
1045   *will last forevermore. All-seeing Zeus*
        and Destiny, unite to seal our truce.
        Raise the hallowed cry, join our blessing song!

        (Exit all as the procession is led offstage. Athena stands in the
        doorway as the doors are finally closed.)

-END-

End: This final stage direction can only be speculative, but the sight of
the procession leading out of the orchestra leaving Athena on stage
framed by the door of the scene building makes for a visually powerful
climax to the trilogy.

Selected Bibliography

Commentaries

Conacher, D. J. 1987. *Aeschylus' Oresteia: A Literary Commentary*. University of Toronto Press: Toronto and London.

Denniston, J. D., and D. L. Page. 1957. *Aeschylus' Agamemnon*. Oxford University Press: Oxford.

Fraenkel, E. 1950. *Aeschylus' Agamemnon*. 3 vols. Oxford University Press: Oxford.

Garvie, A. 1986. *Choephoroi*. Oxford University Press: Oxford.

Headlam, W. G., and Thomson, G. 1938. *The Oresteia of Aeschylus*, 2 vols. Cambridge University Press: Cambridge.

Hogan, J. C. 1984. *A Commentary on the Complete Tragedies of Aeschylus*. University of Chicago Press: Chicago.

Lloyd-Jones, H. 1993. *Oresteia*. University of California Press: Berkeley and Los Angeles.

Podlecki. A. 1987. *Eumenides*. Aris and Phillips: Warminster.

Sommerstein, A. 1989. *Eumenides*. Cambridge University Press: Cambridge.

Other Translations

Fagles, R. 1966. *Aeschylus: The Oresteia*. Viking Press: New York.

Grene, D., and W. Doniger O'Flaherty. 1989. *The Oresteia by Aeschylus*. University of Chicago Press: Chicago and London.

Harrison, T. 1981. *The Oresteia*. Rex Collings: London.

Lattimore, R., in *Aeschylus I*. ed. D. Grene and R. Lattimore. University of Chicago Press: Chicago.

Vellacott, P. 1974. *Aeschylus: The Oresteia*. Penguin: Harmondsworth.

Books and Articles

Bamberger, J. 1974. "The Myth of Matriarchy." In M. Rosaldo and L. Lamphere, eds. *Woman, Culture and Society*, pp. 263–80. Stanford University Press: Stanford, Calif.

Betensky, A. 1978. "Aeschylus' *Oresteia*: the Power of Clytemnestra." *Ramus* 7: 11–25.

Burian, P. 1997. "Tragedy Adapted for Stages and Screens: the Renaissance to the Present," in P. E. Easterling, ed. *The Cambridge Companion to Greek Tragedy*, pp. 228–83. Cambridge University Press: Cambridge.

Chiasson, C. C. 1988. "Lecythia and the Justice of Zeus in Aeschylus' *Oresteia*." *Phoenix* 42: 1–21.

Chioles, J. 1995. *Aeschylus: Mythic Theatre and Voice*. University of Athens Publications: Athens.

Csapo, E., and W. J. Slater. 1995. *The Context of Ancient Drama*. University of Michigan Press: Ann Arbor.

Dodds, E. R. 1960. "Morals and Politics in the *Oresteia*." *Proceedings of the Cambridge Philological Society* 186: 19–31.

Dover, K. J. 1957. "The Political Aspects of Aeschylus' *Eumenides*." *Journal of Hellenic Studies* 77: 230–37.

———. 1973. "Some Neglected Aspects of Agamemnon's Dilemma." *Journal of Hellenic Studies* 93: 58–69.

Easterling, P. E. 1973. "Presentation of Character in Aeschylus." *Greece and Rome* 20: 3–19.

Edwards, M. W. 1977. "Agamemnon's Decision: Freedom and Folly in Aeschylus." *California Studies in Classical Antiquity* 10: 17–38.

Faraone, C. A. 1985. "Aeschylus (*Eum.* 306) and the Attic Judicial Curse Tablets." *Journal of Hellenic Studies* 105: 150–54.

Foley, H. P. 2001. *Female Acts in Greek Tragedy*. Princeton University Press: Princeton.

Gagarin, M. 1975. "The Vote of Athena." *American Journal of Philology* 96: 121–27.

———. 1976. *Aeschylean Drama.* University of California Press: Berkeley and Los Angeles.

Gantz, T. 1993. *Early Greek Myth: A Guide to Literary and Artistic Sources.* Johns Hopkins University Press: Baltimore and London.

Goldhill, S. 1984. *Language, Sexuality, Narrative: The Oresteia.* Cambridge University Press: Cambridge.

———. 1986. *Reading Greek Tragedy.* Cambridge University Press: Cambridge.

———. 1992. *Aeschylus: The Oresteia.* Cambridge University Press: Cambridge.

Gould, J. 1978. "Dramatic Character and 'Human Intelligibility' in Greek Tragedy." *Proceedings of the Cambridge Philological Society* 24: 43–67.

Griffith, M. 1995. "Brilliant Dynasts: Power and Politics in the *Oresteia.*" *Classical Antiquity* 14.1: 63–129.

Halliwell, S. 1997. "Tragedy and Athenian Rhetoric," in C. Pelling, ed. *Greek Tragedy and the Historian,* pp. 121–42. Oxford University Press: Oxford.

Hammond, N. G. L. 1965. "Personal Freedom and Its Limitations in the *Oresteia.*" *Journal of Hellenic Studies* 85: 47–55.

Harris, G. 1973. "Furies, Witches and Mothers," in J. Goody, ed., *The Character of Kinship,* pp. 149–59. Cambridge University Press: Cambridge.

Hartigan, K. V. 1995. *Greek Tragedy and the American Stage: Ancient Drama in the Commerical Theater, 1882–1994.* Greenwood Press: Westport, Connecticut.

Headlam, W. 1906. "The Last Scene of *Eumenides.*" *Journal of Hellenic Studies* 26: 268–77.

Herington, C. J. 1963. "The Influence of Old Comedy on Aeschylus' Later Trilogies." *Transactions and Proceedings of the American Philological Association* 94: 113–25.

———. 1965. "Aeschylus: the Last Phase." *Arion* 4.3: 387–403.

———. 1986. *Aeschylus.* Yale University Press: New Haven.

Hester, D. A. 1981. "The Casting Vote." *American Journal of Philology* 102: 265–74.

Jones, J. 1962. *On Aristotle and Greek Tragedy*. Chatto and Windus: London.

Kitto, H. D. F. 1956. *Form and Meaning in Greek Drama*. Methuen: London.

———. 1961. *Greek Tragedy*. Methuen: London.

Knox, B. M. W. 1952. "The Lion in the House." *Classical Philology* 47: 17-25.

———. 1972. "Aeschylus and the Third Actor." *American Journal of Philology* 93: 104–24. Repr. in *Word and Action: Essays on the Ancient Theatre*. Johns Hopkins University Press: Baltimore 1979. 27–38 and 39–55.

Kuhns, R. 1962. *The House, the City and the Judge: The Growth of Moral Awareness in the Oresteia*. Bobbs-Merrill: Indianapolis.

Lawler, L. B. 1964. *The Dance of Ancient Greek Theater*. A&C Black: London.

Lebeck, A. 1971. *The Oresteia: A Study in Language and Structure*. Harvard University Press: Cambridge, Mass.

Lesky, A. 1966. "Decision and Responsibility in the Tragedy of Aeschylus." *Journal of Hellenic Studies* 86: 78–85.

Lloyd-Jones, H. 1956. "Zeus in Aeschylus." *Journal of Hellenic Studies* 76: 55–67.

———. 1971. *The Justice of Zeus*. University of California Press: Berkeley and Los Angeles.

———. 1983. "Artemis and Iphigenia." *Journal of Hellenic Studies* 103: 87–102.

Macintosh, F. 1977. "Tragedy and Performance: Nineteenth-and-Twentieth-Century Productions." in P. E. Easterling, ed. *The Cambridge Companion to Greek Tragedy*, pp. 284–323. Cambridge University Press: Cambridge.

Macleod, C. 1982. "Politics and the Oresteia." *Journal of Hellenic Studies* 102: 124–44. Repr. in *Collected Essays*. Oxford University Press: Oxford 1983. 20–40.

McCall, M. 1972. *Aeschylus*. Prentice-Hall: Englewood Cliffs, N. J.

McClure, L. 1997a. "Clytemnestra's Binding Spell (*Ag.* 958–74)." *Classical Journal* 92: 123–40.

————. 1997b. "Logos Gunaikos: Speech, Gender, and Spectatorship in the *Oresteia*." *Helios* 24.2:112–35.

————. 1999. *Spoken Like a Woman: Speech and Gender in Athenian Drama*. Princeton University Press: Princeton.

McDonald, M. 1992. *Ancient Sun, Modern Light: Greek Drama on the Modern Stage*. Columbia University Press: New York.

Meier, C. 1993. *The Political Art of Greek Tragedy*. Johns Hopkins University Press: Baltimore.

Nussbaum, M. 1986. *The Fragility of Goodness*. Cambridge University Press: Cambridge.

Peradotto, J. J. 1964. "Some Patterns of Nature Imagery in the *Oresteia*." *American Journal of Philology* 85: 378–93.

————. 1969. "Cledonomancy in the *Oresteia*." *American Journal of Philology* 90: 1–21.

Pickard-Cambridge, A. W. 1968. Second edition revised by J. Gould and D. M. Lewis. *The Dramatic Festivals of Athens*. Oxford University Press: Oxford.

Podlecki, A. J. 1965. *The Political Background of Aeschylean Tragedy*. University of Michigan Press: Ann Arbor.

Prag, A. J. N. W. 1985. *The Oresteia: Iconographic and Narrative Tradition*. Warminster and Bolchazy-Carducci: Chicago.

Rabinowitz, N. S. 1981. "From Force to Persuasion: Aeschylus' *Oresteia* as Cosmogonic Myth." *Ramus* 10: 159–91.

Rehm, R. 1992. *Greek Tragic Theatre*. Routledge: New York and London.

Rosenbloom, D. 1995. "Myth, History, and Hegemony in Aeschylus," in B. Goff, ed., *History, Tragedy, Theory*, pp. 91–130. University of Texas Press: Austin.

Rosenmeyer, T. 1982. *The Art of Aeschylus*. University of California Press: Berkeley and Los Angeles.

Scott, W. C. 1984. *Musical Design in Aeschylean Theater*. University Press of New England: Hanover, N. H.

Seaford, R. 1995. "Historicizing Tragic Ambivalence: The Vote of Athena," in B. Goff, ed., *History, Tragedy, Theory: Dialogues on Greek Drama*, University of Texas Press: Austin.

Simon, E. 1982. *The Ancient Theater*. Methuen: London and New York.

Solmsen, F. 1949. *Hesiod and Aeschylus*. Cornell University Press: Ithaca, N. Y.

Taplin, O. 1977. *The Stagecraft of Aeschylus*. Oxford University Press: Oxford.

———. 1989. *Greek Fire*. Jonathan Cape: London.

Trendall, A. D., and T. B. L. Webster. 1971. *Illustrations of Greek Drama*. Phaidon: London.

Vidal-Naquet, P. 1988. "Hunting and Sacrifice in Aeschylus' *Oresteia*," in J.-P. Vernant and P. Vidal-Naquet, *Myth and Tragedy in Ancient Greece*, pp. 141–60. Trans. J. Lloyd. Zone Books: New York.

West, M. L. 1992. *Ancient Greek Music*. Oxford University Press: Oxford.

Whallon, W. 1980. *Problem and Spectacle: Studies in the Oresteia*. Winter: Heidelberg.

Wiles, D. 1997. *Tragedy in Athens: Performance Space and Theatrical Meaning*. Cambridge University Press: Cambridge.

Winnington-Ingram, R. P. 1948. "Clytemnestra and the Vote of Athena." *Journal of Hellenic Studies* 68: 130–47. Repr. in *Studies in Aeschylus*. Cambridge University Press: Cambridge 1983. 101–31.

Wohl, V. 1998. *Intimate Commerce: Exchange, Gender and Subjectivity in Greek Tragedy*. University of Texas Press: Austin.

Zeitlin, F. 1965. "The Motif of the Corrupted Sacrifice in Aeschylus' *Oresteia*." *Transactions and Proceedings of the American Philological Association* 96: 463–508.

———. 1966. "Postscript to Sacrificial Imagery in the *Oresteia*." *Transactions and Proceedings of the American Philological Association* 97: 645–53.

———. 1978. "The Dynamics of Misogyny: Myth and Mythmaking in the *Oresteia*." *Arethusa* 11: 149–84. Rev. in *Playing the Other*. University of Chicago Press: Chicago 1996. 341–74.